After a Fashion

Joanne Finkelstein

MELBOURNE UNIVERSITY PRESS

Melbourne University Press
PO Box 278, Carlton South, Victoria 3053, Australia

First published 1996
Reprinted 1998

Designed by Mark Davis/text-art
Typeset by Melbourne University Press in 10.5/13 pt Garamond
Printed in Malaysia by SRM Production Services Sdn Bhd

ISSN 1039-6128   391.09 FIN

National Library of Australia Cataloguing-in-Publication entry

Finkelstein, Joanne.
  After a fashion.

  Bibliography.
  Includes index.
  ISBN 0 522 84619 X.

  1. Fashion—Social aspects. 2. Body image—Social
  aspects. 3. Fashion—Psychological aspects. 4. Body
  image—Psychological aspects. I. Title. (Series:
  Interpretations).
391

Contents

1

Introduction

After all, what is fashion? It is usually a form of ugliness so intolerable that we have to alter it every six months.

Oscar Wilde

On 27 January 1995, on the fiftieth anniversary of the liberation of the Nazi concentration camp at Auschwitz in Poland, the Paris fashion house Comme des Garçons launched its menswear collection in the Place Vendôme. The theme of the fashion show was sleep, but when two tall, emaciated young men with closely shaved heads appeared on the catwalk, wearing dressing gowns and striped pyjamas bearing numbers, the striking resemblance to the uniforms of the concentration camps was decried by the world press. The fashion show had opened on the same day that those who had perished in the Holocaust were being commemorated in ceremonies throughout Europe and the rest of the world. In the same week, designer Bernard Perris (of the fashion house Jean-Louis Scherrer) had also been castigated in the press for employing World War II iconography, especially Nazi insignia, in his couture collection, which had featured Gestapo-like caps adorned with an iron cross similar to that used by the German military. These apparently deliberate gestures towards images of neo-Nazi tailoring were described in the international press as unspeakably tasteless. The designer of the Comme des Garçons pyjamas, Rei Kawakubo, was reported as being dismayed at the furore her collection had created. She claimed her show was unfortunate in its timing, but not intended to give offence. This incident was reminiscent of the fiasco created in 1994 by Chanel's Karl Lagerfeld, when his tight, low-cut dress bodices, which featured Koranic verses embroidered in grey pearls, offended many in the Muslim community. After press reports of the reaction, the garments were not permitted to go on sale; indeed, they were destroyed. Like Lagerfeld, Kawakubo also withdrew her garments from sale.

The international press picked up these incidents, as it has other fashion campaigns, and used them to engender an atmosphere of moral outrage. When Rei Kawakubo launched the Comme des Garçons label in Paris in the early 1980s with a collection inscribed as post-Hiroshima, the bruised make-up and powder scattered on the clothes were declared distasteful. When Zandra Rhodes was invited by the Indian Government in 1982 to use and promote local fabrics, she reworked the traditional sari, ripping it and giving it shredded edges. The mutilated sari was seen as an insult. A recent winter collection of Comme des Garçons featured models wrapped in what appeared to be army blankets and fatigue jackets, torn and worn as if from sleeping rough. In his catwalk parades, Versace has frequently played Phil Collins's popular song about a destitute girl living on the streets, 'Paradise', to accompany models clad in clothes worth tens of thousands of dollars. Dolce e Gabbana, the Italian fashion house, dressed its models in slick, chic and natty sharp suits reminiscent of American gangsters of the 1930s at a time when the Italian community was absorbing the murders of judges and police investigators working to bring the Mafia to justice. These allusions to fascism, poverty, dislocation and violence in a Europe not only concerned about its undeclared wars in Bosnia and further east but also about its expanding underclass have been regarded by the international media as inexcusably callous.

A repeated image of fashion designers used by the press represents them as living in remote and rarefied environments. Yves Saint Laurent is described as living in a cocoon, shunning any contact with newspapers, radio and television. This isolation, which is now associated with the *haute couture* industries, leads us to expect that every season some designer somewhere will generate a sensation by stumbling into politically sensitive areas. Although *haute couture* has a reputation for often being sensational and shocking, the political insensitivity evidenced by Lagerfeld, Perris, Kawakubo and others is seen as a new dimension. The shock tactics of *haute couture* were fully exploited during the 1960s and 1970s by Vivienne Westwood and Malcolm McLaren, whose London shop on the King's Road—sequentially called Sex, Seditionaries and World's End—offered torn clothes, jewellery made of razor blades, safety pins, chains and S/M paraphernalia. Their kind of sensationalism begins to look quaint in contrast to the post-Hiroshima, neo-Nazi militarisation of the current catwalks. At least, this is the position taken by fashion commentators such as Marion Hume in the *Independent* newspaper, Suzy Menkes in the *International Herald Tribune*, and Lee Yanowitch for Reuters (see Hume, 1995; Yanowitch, 1995a, b).

The reportage of *haute couture* figures fashion as a contested cultural site. Fashion, in the twentieth century, is big business. The production, marketing and consumption of fashionable items creates a vast economic colossus employing millions of people and generating billions of dollars in revenue. At the same time that we accept fashion as a serious economic enterprise, there is a strong contrary intellectual tendency to condemn it as a frivolity that bestows too great an emphasis on the trivial. Fashion is swathed in such anomalies. On the one hand it is regarded as a distraction, a form of playfulness and humour; on the other, it is understood to generate the economic potential to rehabilitate failing businesses and restore commercial respect. Fashion can be used to indicate social change and progress, for example, by weakening the prescriptions around gender-appropriate dress. But at the same time fashion is a conservative influence, as the longevity of the business suit indicates. The numerous anomalies embodied in fashion make it a solid plinth from which to explore the social and cultural forces that shape modern life.

When Fredric Jameson (1990) characterises the modern sensibility as archetypically schizoid because of its powers to compress and to make sense of contradictory images and distorted temporal frames, he could be describing the contemporary fashion *habitué*.

The contradictions expressed through fashion seem to parallel the disturbances, disjunctions and conflicts found in the everyday world. Jameson's modern individual harbours an anarchic, fragmented and protean self, which makes the pursuit of fashion seem a reasonable and potentially satisfying impulse. Indeed, Dick Hebdige's vivid description of the contemporary, fashionable individual alludes to many of these points:

> The ideal consumer as deduced from contemporary advertisements is not a 'he' or a 'she' but an 'it' . . . It is a young but powerful (i.e. solvent) Porsche-owning gender bender who wears Katherine Hamnet skirts and Gucci loafers, watches Dallas on air and Eastenders on video, drinks lager, white wine or Grolsch and Cointreau, uses tampons, smokes St Bruno pipe tobacco, uses Glintz hair colour, cooks nouvelle and eats out at McDonald's, is an international jetsetter who holidays in the Caribbean and lives in a mock-Georgian mansion . . . The ideal consumer is not the ideal productive worker of an earlier epoch—a sexually repressed nobody, alienated from sensual pleasure, subjected to the turgid, life-denying disciplines of the working week and the nuclear family. Instead, the ideal consumer . . . is a complete social and psychological mess. The ideal consumer as extrapolated from the barrage of contradictory interpellations from advertising billboards to magazine spreads to TV commercials is a bundle of conflicting drives, desires, fantasies, appetites . . . The subject of advertising is not the rational sovereign subject of Descartes . . . it is Deleuze and Guattari's 'body without organs'—the absolute decentred subject, the irresponsible, unanchored subject: the psychotic consumer, the schizophrenic consumer. (Hebdige, 1993:82–3)

Fashion is often considered one of those social forces which keeps us ever attentive to the present in one of the worst possible ways; that is, as a source of novelty, distraction, and self-absorption. Fashion—and this is in relation to material items such as clothing as well as ideas and practices—seems to be about individuality, about standing out from the crowd. It seems to be about change, the constant unravelling of the new and the display of the inventive. But often its effect is the reverse: it maintains the status quo and encourages conformity and uniformity. On closer examination, fashion is about turbulence and creating a sense of movement without pointing in any direction. 'The chief characteristic of fashion', writes Renato Poggioli, 'is to impose and suddenly to accept as a new rule or norm what was, until a minute before, an exception or whim, then to abandon it again after it has become a commonplace, everybody's "thing"' (1968:79).

Fashion has the effect of making an idea or commodity or aesthetic perspective into a seemingly inclusive category. Suddenly, everyone knows and understands that this is the cutting edge, this is where the action is, this is valuable. The apparent instantaneousness of fashion lends it an attractive volatility. Fashion is regarded as the site where we come into immediate contact with human creativity, for it signifies the intervention of a dominating human mind. At the same time, fashion has a subaltern or alternative function which is so submerged and implicit that it comes as a shock. As Poggioli suggests, fashion is really about maintaining the eternal sameness, preserving the status quo; it is a quixotic gesture, a con trick, a sleight of hand, which makes us think change is happening when the opposite is closer to the truth. Poggioli's allusion to the rapid turnover of what is fashionable alerts us to this. Fashions are not about putting into circulation the really new, because the genuine novelty cannot be absorbed quickly into the cultural formations of everyday life. Fashion—in its various guises as a practice, an industry and a social force—provides no such opportunity for a full engagement with the new. Fashions are continuously being recycled, and new marketing strategies are constantly being tried out to maintain this impetus.

The constancy of circulation, whether in ideas or material goods, indicates that the actual function of fashion is to give the appearance of change and novelty without actually precipitating any ruptures to the status quo. A fashion is generally thought of as a prevailing custom or mannerism for specific groups. Because it is a hybrid phenomenon, located in the interstices between economics and art, psychology and commerce, creativity and banality, it has captured the attention of various commentators and theorists. They have characterised fashion as a social, economic and aesthetic force, and, more often than not, all three at the same time. Throughout this book, the word 'fashion' is used to encompass these simultaneous applications. While fashion is commonly attached to clothes and appearances, it would be misleading to think of it only in this regard. As the title *After a Fashion* suggests, there are other considerations which take the idea of fashion beyond material goods. Striving after a fashion, for instance, is to pursue an ideal often with the understanding that it is unattainable. To act or behave after a fashion implies a slight deviation or imperfection, as if something were not quite fulfilled, as if an achievement were not of sufficient standard. After a fashion suggests a space between the desired and the performed, and it is with these additional nuances that the term fashion is used here.

The idea of fashion has been in circulation for a long time, and there are numerous ways of thinking about it. Economic historians, anthropologists, literary theorists, psychologists and sociologists have each made their distinctive forays into fashion. The *Annales* historian, Fernand Braudel, dates the origins of the modern idea of fashion to early capitalism, to the bazaars and itinerant traders who traversed Europe in the sixteenth century. He regards fashion largely as an economic phenomenon. Other perspectives explain fashion through aesthetic, sexual, social and psychological formulations. The psychological perspective, which began with J. C. Flügel (1930) and has recently been rearticulated by Alison Lurie (1992), treats consumer behaviour and psychology as mutually revealing. Psychologists may well say that one is what one buys, owns, displays, desires; the contours of the psyche are written on the surface of the body, in one's style of dress as well as one's language, manners of sociability and sexual practices. Fashion, from a psychological point of view, has been described as a form of exhibitionism: at the same time that it conceals the body it also exaggerates its differences, and thereby creates a constant tension between the rival desires to display oneself and to retain a sense of modesty.

To imbue goods with psychological and sexual properties in addition to their economic value is to naturalise culturally specific styles of conduct and norms of behaviour. The various effects of fashion—on economic activity, social and sexual mores, aesthetic and psychological formations—strongly suggest that any analysis of it needs to recognise these complex and paradoxical influences. Consequently, fashion must be looked at from several angles, such as a history of body decoration and costume, a language and form of irrational play, an expression of sexuality, an economic event, and an urban experience. A comprehensive look at fashion involves seeing it as a globalising and culturally homogenising phenomenon, as the impetus behind international advertising, *haute couture* and big business, as well as a gimmick which sustains vast economic structures such as shopping malls and world trade expositions. In the name of fashion, a multitude of influences can be seen at work, and these affect the ways people think and act both privately and publicly. This book surveys various perspectives of fashion in order to outline the questions, manners of thinking and conclusions fashion has provoked.

2

The Elusive Origins
of Fashion

*And the eyes of Adam and Eve were opened, and they knew that
they were naked; and they sewed fig leaves together, and made
themselves aprons.*

Genesis 3:7

Although fashion is taken for granted as a naturalised part of
everyday life, it occupies a contested site in the cultural field. It is
the ubiquity of fashion that helps make it seem so natural. Because
every western society appears to have some form of fashion, this
makes it seem unremarkable. Various accounts of the origins of
fashion reinforce this view. Diverse and vague, they eschew explanation, concentrating instead on what is understood as the
easier project, namely, the chronicling of specific fashion details.
This is precisely how the well-known historians of fashion, Max
von Boehn (1932), James Laver (1969a), and Quentin Bell (1976)
approach the topic. Offering little in the way of explanation, their
works are highly detailed descriptions of who wore what when.

Whenever explanations of fashion are offered they commonly
link the psychological with the biological, thereby making
fashion appear to originate in a universal human desire for social
approval, acceptance and individuality. Framing fashion as a
psycho-biological gesture overcomes the difficulty of accounting
for its variety. Following this logic, no matter what form fashion
takes, it remains an expression of fundamental human needs to

decorate and to promote oneself. Such psychological explanations also allow for the imputation of various motives to those who value fashion. For instance, Quentin Bell (1976) begins his exploration of fashion with the assertion that individuals interested in fashion must be irrational or gullible or both, because to maintain one's fashionability one must act in a most irrational manner, namely, spending too much time and money on an elusive goal:

> It is true of dress in even a higher degree than of most other items of consumption, that people will undergo a very considerable degree of privation in the comforts or necessities of life in order to afford what is considered a decent amount of wasteful consumption. (Thorstein Veblen quoted in Bell, 1976:15)

Bell's supposedly rational but decontextualised point of view represents fashion as a measure of human stupidity and gullibility. Accordingly, Bell finds it remarkable that people would willingly go ill clad in order to appear fashionably well dressed. He gives as an example the wearing of skimpy, sometimes damp and clinging negligees for evening wear, a fashion once favoured by nineteenth-century, upper-class women. He also considers it irrational to imagine that to appear in fashionable clothing will improve one's good reputation, when being fashionable means overlooking the serviceableness of the garments themselves. Bell here draws on the earlier work, *A Theory of the Leisure Class* (1899) by Thorstein Veblen.

As an economic rationalist, Veblen regarded functional simplicity as the highest aesthetic attainment. The impractical, the excessive and the sumptuous seemed ugly to him. Nor did he appreciate the relativity of beauty, in so far as what appears ugly or beautiful at one moment can be perceived differently at another time. Fashion and the pursuit of new aesthetic styles thus struck Veblen as nonsensical, and for this reason utterly fascinating. His study of the late nineteenth-century leisure classes was impassioned by his desire to explain the conduct of those newly enriched individuals who were untiringly interested in conspicuous display and the pursuit of the fashionable. His account of fashion—

which gives priority to notions of rivalry, class differentiation, competition, and the petty struggle to gain prestige and better one's social status—resonates with psychological assumptions about human nature. While Veblen understood fashion to be largely an economic phenomenon, it seemed to originate in an inexplicable human urge for self-adornment and decorative costuming. This point of view again emphasises the irrational, especially when specific fashions fail to be aesthetically pleasing. Bell also adopts this position when he states that 'clothes hurt us in a pecuniary, a physical, an aesthetic and frequently a moral sense; they are (very often) expensive, unhealthy, ugly and immodest' (1976:21). The irrationality of fashion turns clothes into the 'monstrous and absurd' (ibid.:17).

Veblen's account of fashion has endured for decades, and his idea of the circulation of fashion, often referred to as the 'trickle-down effect' (a phrase he himself does not use), is continually referenced in the literature. Veblen's theory emphasises the economic aspects of fashion by treating it as a mechanism for demonstrating wealth. At the same time, however, the wish to display wealth and success emanates from a more subterranean desire to demonstrate superiority. Veblen regards fashion as an invention of the upper classes, designed to distinguish them from those below. When their styles and practices were imitated, when their fashions 'trickled down' to their social inferiors, the upper classes were impelled to reconstitute themselves with a different aesthetic. Thus fashion became a socially acceptable mechanism for expressing the rivalry, competition and conflict which always existed between the different social strata. Fashion was a way not only of distinguishing individuals but also of positioning them in a social hierarchy.

Veblen's analysis is specific to the new industrial era and its shifting formations of social class. He focuses on the acute self-consciousness that individuals experienced in a society where mobility caused social position to fluctuate. Many of the social transactions engaged in by the upwardly mobile were thus designed to demonstrate conspicuous consumption, conspicuous leisure and conspicuous waste in order to assert social identity and location. Fashion was a means of self-posturing, and of ameliorating the competitive rivalry inherent in the new social order. According to Veblen, displays of rare and highly valued commodities such as *haute couture*, furs, precious metals and gems, were necessarily conspicuous because this was the technique for claiming an elevated social position. When such garments were copied and made more cheaply, they became available to the lower classes and thus lost their exclusivity and value. Veblen understood why the upper classes had to be the prime developers of fashion. Needing to differentiate themselves from those below, from those who were always imitating them, they created the impetus for a continuous cycle of new fashion.

Fashionability was regarded as an effective measure of wealth because it required the individual to have a great deal of leisure. Veblen describes the fashions of the upper classes in terms of how much time was required to create them, and how much leisure time they consumed in order to be properly displayed. Hats, for example, were measures of wealth and conspicuous leisure because they were difficult to wear; often a liability outdoors, they offered little protection from the weather, and were often shown to their best advantage in sequestered social settings. Elaborate hair-styles were another instance of conspicuous leisure, as were the wearing of heavy jewellery, clothes with large draping sleeves, high-heeled shoes, and the enamelling of finger-nails. In some quarters, these are still used as signs of wealth, because they require time and effort to prepare and to wear to full effect.

Perhaps the most spectacular claims of social position are made through conspicuous waste. Such gestures have not been confined to the industrialised west, with its overproduction of consumer goods. Conspicuous waste is to be observed in the ritual potlatch associated with both the Kwakiutl Indians of British Columbia and the moka ceremonial exchange of the Mount Hagen tribes in New Guinea. The potlatch is a ritual wasting; it bestows great social status on the individual who is able to give away, destroy and recklessly endanger the community's most important treasures. In western societies, displays of perishables such as freshly cut flowers and food, one-off spectacles like the opening nights of concerts, theatre and opera, funerals, weddings, and the keeping of pets (especially those that are exotic and require expensive, special care) can all be taken as instances of conspicuous waste.

Veblen's theory of fashion is a study of social inequality. Fashion is a mechanism for articulating social position. Fashionable consumer goods are used to differentiate oneself from others who are deemed inferior, and to promote association with those regarded as one's peers. But fashion, as a social status, is also anomalous and unpredictable. While everyone knows that fashion is repetitive, superfluous, wasteful and futile, it is also taken seriously. Although often described as a trivial activity, and used to highlight the unattractive human traits of flippancy and gullibility, fashion is also believed to be a means of satisfying certain psychological needs. Bell acknowledges these functions by reference to the eighteenth-century letters of Lord Chesterfield, who instructed his son to understand that while stylish dress may be foolish and an expensive vanity, it is more foolish not to be well dressed, because adherence to fashion encodes other and more important declarations such as allegiance to the social order (Bell, 1976:18).

It is common to regard fashionability as the expression of a willingness to play by the rules and be judged by appearances. Bell modernises this functionalist position by adding that failing to play the game (by wearing the 'wrong' necktie, the 'cheap' perfume, the 'imitation' or look-alike) is worse than not playing at all. Even if those choices are inadvertent—and one wears the wrong tie because one does not know which is the right one—it is still considered to be playing the game badly: indicating failure, a lack of special knowledge, it represents a betrayal of oneself which has been witnessed by others (ibid.:19). Such a position invests fashion with the capacity to measure social respectability: it makes fashion into a sign of morality.

To dress badly, to violate certain codes of sartorial conduct, can be interpreted as a psychological betrayal. Inadvertently, it exposes the gap between personal aspirations and social opportunities. Based on an assumed stability in the social order, such views suggest that dress can undermine social position by exposing dissemblance. In reverse, it can also support the individual's right to claim superiority. The simplicity of this viewpoint has not harmed its popularity. Indeed, it remains in currency because it endorses the ideology of modern democracies which claim that, although the social structure is inherently stable, upward mobility is possible. Fashion supports this ideology. For example, the possibility of using fashion opportunistically is evidenced when parvenus dress in clothes of rank but lack the credentials these garments supposedly represent, or when imitations of high-status commodities (such as those labelled Gucci, Chanel, Dior, Cartier) are passed off as genuine, or when individuals choose to cross-dress and thus represent themselves as members of the opposite sex, or when the gendering of clothes is obviously parodied by cross-overs. Stretching the rules of acceptable dress in order to satisfy personal aspirations can succeed. Hence the value of fashion is reinforced as an effective tool in the social advancement of astute individuals.

Fashion can work at different levels. It can function as a social force, as Veblen notes when he describes how the upper classes continuously reinvent their aesthetics in order to differentiate themselves from their 'inferiors'. Fashion can also operate at an imaginative level in order to match the fantasies of those who employ it to reposition themselves. Fashion is made to appear universal through its ubiquity. It seems capable of meeting psychological needs for self-expression and competitive self-promotion. It can be applied to the performance of social categories such as status, class and gender. It can be recognised in the impulse to decorate the body with ceremonial masks, ritual scarification and permanent tattooing. It is this promiscuity of fashion that readily makes it seem to be a cultural universal. Following up this proposition, Georg Simmel (1904) has argued that fashion can be employed as a measure of the civilising process. The logic behind this manoeuvre is that fashion denotes self-consciousness, and that when the cycles of fashion move rapidly then a more complex idea of self will exist. Simmel, an early twentieth-century social theorist, observes that those who adorn themselves with tattoos and scarification treat their skin and bodies as emblems of themselves, whereas those who use metals and precious stones as jewellery have a more elaborate and attenuated relationship between their identity and their social membership. This difference reflects cultural evolution.

> Everything that 'adorns' man can be ordered along a scale in terms of its closeness to the physical body. The 'closest' adornment is typical of nature peoples: tattooing. The opposite extreme is represented by metal and stone adornments, which are entirely unindividual and can be put on by everybody. (Simmel, 1950:340)

The widespread fascination with body image underscores the idea that a preoccupation with appearances—as evidenced by fashion—is a natural, universalistic tendency. Self-consciousness about the body takes multiple forms. Fashionable clothing is one example; another is an awareness of the rules about body maintenance, self-protection and the need to barricade oneself against external dangers and various threats of pollution (Schilder, 1935; Douglas, 1973). Biologically grounded models for explaining human diversity not only naturalise cultural gestures but also claim to explain many social innovations. For example, the stereoscopic vision of humans (which has enhanced an upright posture, the capacity to look ahead into the distance, and a developed perception of spatial depth) has been treated as a plinth from which social biologists confidently explain the pleasures of looking and of shaping physical environments into the visually arresting. The history of art production, the building of urban landscapes, and human body decoration are all swept together as 'natural' expressions of the human need to aestheticise the environment.

Many of the early twentieth-century explanations of fashion have emerged from this social biology perspective. The inclusiveness of such theories makes it possible to argue that no matter how different styles in clothing and body decoration may be, they are linked as techniques which act as surface barriers to protect the body not only from physical but also from social dangers, such as interclass rivalries and marginalisation. Clothes, decorative masks and rituals of anointing the body thus appear to be universally similar devices for protecting the body and the individual's social identity. Physical features, too, such as height and the distribution of hair, become signs which link the physical body with the social body. Edmund Leach, a structural anthropologist, has argued in his ethnographic essay on 'Magical Hair' (1958) that the management of hair is a ritualised enactment of status control. Hair-cutting is a way of ritualising castration; it signals that changes have taken place in the individual's social-sexual status. For Leach, the link between hair and sexuality in the subconscious makes the gesture of hair management universally interpretable. It is the same with other rituals. While their exact meaning may not always be transparent, the apparent ubiquity of these ritualised and symbolised activities none the less signals the existence of commonly asserted linkages between body image, personal identity and cultural forms such as fashion.

Styles of dress are simultaneously intimate and public; they have a sensuous appeal to the wearer while at the same time addressing the world at large. This capacity to bridge the divide between interior and exterior has imputed to fashion an ability to reveal the invisible. The early psychoanalyst, J. C. Flügel (1930), reads clothes in these terms as the indicators of sexual transaction. Clothes sexualise appearance by stimulating the erotic imagination; the shapes of garments, their emphases on different parts of the body, the acts of taking off and putting on clothes, are all tinged with sexual satisfactions. Flügel explains the attraction of the high-heeled shoe in terms of its ability to intensify the sensuality of the female body by reproportioning it. The elevated shoe lengthens the body, slants the hips to make the bottom protrude, and flattens the stomach. The heel itself he treats as a phallic symbol. But Flügel's analysis is flawed by his focus on twentieth-century women. He overlooks not only the use of high heels by men in previous centuries, but also the fact that the high heel has gone cyclically in and out of fashion over the years (Bell, 1976:95).

Irrespective of the success of fashion in bridging the antique problem of mind and body, its value is often assumed to rest here. Simultaneously, fashion is thought of as connecting the inner and private realms of subjectivity (where the unfettered imagination can fantasise about appearance) with the public domain of conventions, codes of conduct, and regulation, where appearances are taken to represent the invisible world of personality. In a cryptic comment, Bell acknowledges the capacity of fashion to cross from interior to exterior worlds: 'If we attempt to correlate the ethical, religious, political or aesthetic ideas of men and women with the clothes that they wear and have worn . . . [then] fashion is what it is because the Zeitgeist makes it so' (Bell, 1976:102).

Fashion appears to be located also at the intersection of the private and public in so far as it produces a visual culture. Clothes are regarded as the visible manifestation of entire systems of value. This has been the logic behind those sumptuary laws which make social rank visible by determining exactly what luxury items or styles of dress an individual may own. Sumptuary laws have existed in almost every society at one time or another. Von Boehn (1932), in his four-volume *Modes and Manners,* Norbert Elias (1978, 1983), in his history of court society and manners, and Rosalind Williams (1982), in her study of the department store and consumer culture, all itemise instances of sumptuary laws at work in various settings. Farid Chenoune (1993) reports a recent instance of the breaching of a sumptuary restriction, when in 1943 the American marines were called in to Los Angeles to quell rioting zoot-suiters, whose offence was the ostentatious waste of cloth during wartime rationing. The sight of so many zoot-suiters in oversized garments apparently provoked angry responses from others who felt disadvantaged by economic stringencies. Sumptuary laws attempt to regulate the ownership and display of specified styles of clothing and adornment. Often these laws are designed to protect home industries by regulating the use of imported fabrics and items, but most are directed at the preservation of class structures and social privilege. A great deal of legislation concerning tariff agreements, favoured trade practices and international alliances continues to accumulate around such laws. Fashion, after all, was and remains a form of big business. GATT, the General Agreement on Tariffs and Trade, could be called a set of sumptuary laws.

Fashions produce a visual culture in which individuals become more self-conscious of their own appearance and that of others. As the art historian Anne Hollander has argued, 'most people do care very deeply about the way their clothes look, although they may not care about fashion, do not spend much time shopping, or do not have large wardrobes or much money and leisure' (1980:347). Fashion is defined by Hollander as 'the whole spectrum of desirable ways of looking at any given time. The scope of what everyone wants to be seen wearing in a given society is what is in fashion; and this includes *haute couture*, all forms of anti-fashion and nonfashion—a periodically fashionable attitude in the history of dress' (ibid.:350).

Hollander's definition is important because it recognises that styles and fashions in clothes and appearances are influential, whether they are official or acts of disavowal. It includes those who imagine they can resist fashion through signs of counter-cultural rebellion. Hollander dismisses this gesture as misguided; it signals that the anti-fashionable have failed to understand how pervasive fashion is in the styling of everyday life, and that anti-fashion is another name for fashion. By influencing not only the definition of shapes and colours but also the reciprocal visual relations with various parts of the body, fashion may seem highly unstable and constantly shifting, but this is how it draws people into its orbit even when they think they are ignoring it (ibid.).

In *Seeing Through Clothes* (1980) Hollander interprets the role of costume in western culture, and suggests that the ways in which dress is ordinarily seen set the boundaries of normalcy, so that what is perceived is influenced largely by artistic representations of the human form. Her argument employs the canon of western painting and sculpture to show how people see through images, and assert their differences and social privileges in the ways they disport themselves. Hollander makes the point that no matter how influential the history of portraiture and classical painting has been in the past, the present era is dominated by an unprecedented visual pluralism created by photo-journalism, the cinema and advertising (ibid.:345). The mass-circulated, techno-logically reproduced image seems to have an unlimited reach. Innovations in photographic, cinematic and computer imaging continue to question the correspondence between what is seen and what is accepted as normal. In studies of the fashion photograph, Brookes (1992) and Triggs (1992) have pointed out independently that this kind of photography, which was once a disparaged practice, is now responsible for those images which order and aestheticise the everyday. Hollander anticipates this position when she comments that 'the tyranny of fashion itself has in fact never been stronger than in this period of visual pluralism . . . The question now is not how to dress suitably for a given event according to certain social rules or how to be in fashion but, rather, what fashion to be in, how to dress so as to indicate that one has the correct perspective on its particular rules' (ibid.).

Hollander draws some support for her argument from a tacitly psycho-biological premise. In the late twentieth century, she believes, perception is different. The eye takes in different details and colours largely because technology is so pervasive: 'people simply saw less clearly before cinematic close-ups and snapshot photography taught everyone to observe each other with sharper eyes than centuries of drawing, painting and engraving had done' (ibid.:346). The result has been a more acute capacity to interpret the most simple and subtle of signs in the ways people dress. It is an argument partially anticipated by Roland Barthes (1985) who analyses fashion as a system of meaning constructed from visual and linguistic details.

In the age of mass production, clothing itself has become more varied in some regards and more similar in others, and so the interpretation of it is based on different assumptions. Clothing no longer designates class, rank and occupation unequivocally; indeed, 'dressing to make ambiguous one's exact identity is a very common game' (ibid.:347). For Hollander, the reading of fashion, in the late twentieth century, has become remarkably complex:

> every tiny choice of texture, color, and shape has a connotation. All methods and degrees of expressing formality and casualness, and all varieties of sexual emphasis, make oblique references to the groups, subgroups, current ideologies, movies, movements, historical periods, or individuals with which they are associated; everything makes reference to an image . . . Acuity of perception about clothes has sharpened under the

stimulation of multiple choice. Distinctions are much finer. (ibid.:345–6)

As a result, Hollander maintains that the diversity in clothing makes its function harder to understand. Nowadays jeans can be exclusively designed or mass manufactured, and both styles are very popular. Some T-shirts sell for one dollar and others for fifty dollars; they can simultaneously suggest 'regional origin, social style, sexual and moral outlook, attitudes toward work, money, leisure, and pleasure, and, above all, the other people one's clothes associate one with' (ibid.:347). The profound importance to us of visuality as a means of reading one another is further emphasised in Hollander's 1994 analysis of men's fashion, which interprets the stability of the business suit as a sign of men's dread of looking foolish. In short, fashions in clothes amplify the social significance of appearances.

Hollander rehearses the commonplace view that fashion is the natural expression of those with a certain flair, and which originates with individuals who are artistic enough to work visually. Fashion, in other words, is the result of the *haute couturier*, who is always an artist. The idea that designers are artists was a mid-nineteenth century French invention which enabled the dress designer to be deemed an original genius, much like the painter. The great couturiers thus gained reputations for being above commercial influences, and as having purely aesthetic visions unmodified by client demands or public responses (ibid.:351–2). Dressmakers, tailors and textile workers, who were formerly anonymous and relegated to the inferior sphere of 'mechanical' arts, changed their status in the nineteenth century and became 'artists of luxury', poets, aesthetes and arbiters of elegance. It should be pointed out that it was men not women who enjoyed this new status. Charles Frederick Worth, for instance, is memorialised for having elevated fashion into an aesthetic. It is 'from Worth's day on [that] couturiers enjoyed unprecedented prestige. They were recognised as poets' (Lipovetsky, 1994:66). This mythology of fashion still exists, in some quarters.

In the twentieth century, the fashion garment industry has been dominated by women: it is mostly women who make clothes in factories, sell them through department stores and boutiques, and shop for clothes. However, as an enterprise, the fashion world still seems controlled by prominent men, such as Karl Lagerfeld at Chanel, Yves Saint Laurent, Pierre Cardin, Christian Dior and Cristobel Balenciaga. The names of female fashion designers from the late nineteenth century to the present—Jeanne Lanvin, Madame Paquin, Madelaine Vionnet, and Sonia Rykiel—do not come to mind so readily.

In the century after Worth, *haute couturiers* became famous because they clothed other famous people, and in particular actresses (Hollander, 1980:354). Dress design had become a separate art available to whoever could afford it. Fashion was no longer restricted to the great high-ranking, public personages with their unique style of appearance. It no longer needed a king or queen to popularise a style, although as a marketing strategy this still remains very effective, as the recent examples of Diana, Princess of Wales, and Madonna indicate. Their personal celebrity can popularise dress styles and help create vast fortunes for specific fashion houses (Bordo, 1993; Kellner, 1994).

The historical positioning of the dress designer as artistic, perverse, troublesome, talented and expensive has also contributed to the mid-twentieth century view that fashion embodies a narcissistic, homosexual, misogynist and sometimes villainous attitude to women. Bergler maintains that fashion designers were understood to be homosexual men, who were knowingly inimical toward their potential clients (that is, heterosexual women) because they were in competition with them for male attention. Fashions such as stiletto shoes, tube-mini skirts, and *décolletage* necklines are often physically demanding to wear, and Bergler contends invented by homosexual designers in order to ridicule women and to blunt their competitive edge in the pursuit of heterosexual males (Bergler, 1953:117–20).

This is a contentious claim which Bell, for instance, would dismiss on the grounds that designers are neither powerful nor artists. Bell maintains that no one creates fashion, because markers of social difference, such as clothes, work only in a society where social divisions exist already. He cites the example of Charles II, who in 1666 tried to halt fashion by introducing the vest, after the style of an Oriental-inspired tunic. Since this serviceable garment was in his opinion the perfect item, no other styles would ever need to be developed. Yet although the King and all his court wore the vest, the ambition to halt fashion failed. As Samuel Pepys recorded in his diary on 22 November 1666, Louis XIV (with whom Charles was at war) ordered his footmen to be dressed in the vest, and with this inspired gesture put an end to the Caroline fashion. For by cladding his subordinates in the vaunted vest, Louis executed a parodic victory over Charles which proved more effective than a military campaign. A more contemporary example is the Mao suit which homogenised a nation into a specific look and supplied the west, albeit briefly, with a politically informed style.

Other contradictions in the 'embedded misogyny' theory of fashion are relatively few. Diana Fuss (1992), on the contrary, has argued that contemporary fashion photography tacitly produces a particular gaze or way of seeing which, although it regulates homosexual desire, also gives it opportunities for expression. Fuss analyses the generic features of women's fashion photography through a psychoanalytic understanding of how sexual identity is formed, and from this perspective suggests that the spectatorial relation established between the female image and the female viewer—what she calls the homospectatorial position—activates a homosexual fusion of identification and desire. Fuss approves of this latent function of the fashion enterprise in a way which Bergler would find menacing. Where Bergler is trying to warn us of a homosexual conspiracy which devalues women, Fuss is indicating where unexpected pleasures may be found.

Hollander's approach to fashion, by contrast, is formalist; she sees fashion as a self-enclosed system largely impervious to historical circumstances. She would not attach much significance to Charles's vest or to Louis XIV's use of layered clothing as a political gesture. (Louis XIV dressed in several different layers of clothing—a style also imitated by his courtiers—in order to prolong the court ritual of the royal levee, during which he entertained increasingly important people in the quasi-privacy of his ritualised toilette. The more clothes Louis dropped, the more important the conversation.) Such uses of fashion cannot be accounted for by

Hollander's perceptual history, which depends on the assumption of a basic human need to decorate the body. This underlies her account of why fashion developed into big business, why it seems always to be in motion and presumably progressing to better styles, and why the couturier is best seen as an artist, sculptor or fabric architect who has gone commercial.

Hollander sees appearance as a social transaction which provides personal satisfactions, such as a feeling that one is successful in being upwardly mobile or at the cutting edge. At the same time, however, fashion caters to such imaginings without effecting any real consequences; as dress 'expresses other kinds of classification—age, sex, occupation—obviously a change of clothes can come before or instead of any possible change in circumstance' (Hollander, 1980:355). Clothes and appearances may well indicate the existence of new social configurations and opportunities, but they can also 'suggest, persuade, connote, insinuate, or indeed lie'. To interpret changes in appearance is thus problematic, for clothes can be tools for dissemblance. They allow people 'to try to be other than they [are]: richer, higher born, younger, or of another sex . . . and, of course, beautiful if they [are] really ugly' (ibid.). Just as readily, fashions in appearances may mean none of these. To some extent, the promiscuity of fashion hides its significance.

While much of the early theorising of fashion attempts to link the psychological with the biological in order to make it seem a natural event, recognition must be paid also to fashion as a culturally specific and historically contingent phenomenon. Even when explanations of fashion employ the terminology of the universal—as, for instance, when Bergler formulates fashion in psychoanalytic terms as a transhistorical form of female narcissism and exhibitionism—such generalisations are specific to a particular cultural moment. The origins of fashion as a form of consumption can be located in displays of wealth and success which express unconscious desires associated with rivalry and competition. Fashions in appearances, consumer goods and practices can mediate between the notional needs of an individual and the conventions of a social group. Explanations of dominant styles in appearance, and how they change, cannot be fully accounted for by examining the history of a garment: for instance, how the business suit or necktie evolved cannot be the basis for explaining fashion. Instead, those transformations of appearance which fashion records may be interpreted as signalling ruptures in the perceptual order, and as highlighting changes in the social organisation of values. Our fashioned appearances evince the dominance of the visual, and give material form to that abstract relationship between aesthetic impulses and the desire for social conformity. In short, fashion is a versatile social and psychological mechanism that lacks a fixed point of origin.

3

Speaking of Fashion

Modernity is a code, and fashion is its emblem.

Jean Baudrillard

Fashion theory is frequently punctuated with references to the 'language of clothes', a phrase made popular by Alison Lurie in the early 1980s (Lurie, 1992). This phrase suggests that clothes somehow have the power of articulation, that appearances 'speak'. The metaphor that fashion is a language has persisted despite the obvious failure of clothing to produce the fundamental require- ments of a language, namely, an explicit vocabulary, parts of speech, syntax and dialogue. Clothes do not speak to us or to one another; they do not sustain a system of meaningful exchange. Social encounters constituted by language are unscripted, flexible and unpredictable. Even if, by a generous reckoning, we allow that clothes can 'make a statement', they are not capable of nuanced exchange. While meanings proliferate through human speech, clothing remains static; while words change their meaning only slowly, the fashionability of clothing—and hence the meanings it disseminates—changes every season (Davis, 1992:7–8). To speak of the 'language' of clothes then is to acknowledge the persistence of this metaphor rather than to discover a conventional linguistic system embedded in materials produced by the fashion industry.

Both Hollander (1980) and Lurie (1992) employ the metaphor of clothes as a language. Lurie calls clothes and fashion accessories a 'visual language' with its own grammar, syntax and vocabulary. Her analysis, which sometimes reads like parody, enunciates the exact meanings and aesthetic formations carried by certain images. The red necktie favoured by President Ronald Reagan during the early 1980s, for example, is interpreted as symbolising virility and heterosexuality. In this instance, the ordinary necktie becomes a statement of conventionalised sexual practices. 'A man's tie may also be sexually symbolic', Lurie informs us, 'especially if it is brightly colored or in some way unusual'. In her reading, 'the tieless Catholic priest is "symbolically castrated"', and 'the narrow woven cord or leather thong ties often favored by elderly American men suggest a withering or drying up of the passions' (1992:244–5).

This assumed correspondence between inner and outer spheres suggests that clothing can be used either deliberately to promote oneself to interested on-lookers, or inadvertently to betray one's inner, secret self. Dress maps on to the self, according to Lurie: 'the woman in the sensible grey wool suit and the frilly pink blouse is a serious, hard-working mouse with a frivolous and feminine soul' (ibid.:245). Clothing is a shorthand for social status. Lurie argues:

> the well-to-do can be observed to have on more clothes. The men are more likely to wear vests; the women are more apt to wear panty hose, superfluous scarves and useless little wraps . . . On the beach, though the rich may splash into the waves in suits as skimpy as anyone else's, the moment they emerge they will make a dash for the conspicuous raw-silk beach kimono, terry swim dress or linen shirt that matches their bathing suit and restores the status quo. (ibid.:121)

Although Barthes (1985) and Lévi-Strauss (1972) retain the metaphor of a semiotic system, both recognise that fluidities and ambiguities inherent in the structure of fashionable appearance force its codes to remain open-ended. Lurie remains confident in her interpretations of colours, styles, textures and fabrics; others are more aware of the instability of meaning transmitted through these methods, which include the ways in which clothes are worn, and the body postures that different individuals adopt. This leads the semioticians of fashion to conclude that while fashions obviously speak, it is unclear what they say (Davis, 1992:6). It may be possible to posit some rules, such as that dark colours suggest formality, light colours informality, angularity masculinity, and curvilinear forms femininity, yet for every rule there will immediately appear a series of anomalies. The fact that styles in clothing change quickly—making their status and value hard to locate—supports the view that clothes are a source of unresolved ambiguity.

In his essay on American clothing, the anthropologist Marshall Sahlins (1976:179–204) adopts a structuralist perspective to argue that colour (light or dark), hue (bright or dull), texture (rough or smooth), direction (horizontal or vertical) and line (straight or curved) all serve to encode in clothes the fundamental cultural distinctions of gender, status, age, occupation, lifestyle, ethnicity, and sexuality, and they do so in ways which are largely unrecognised and unconscious. He maintains that the visuality of clothes enables them to express specific binary opposites, such as being chaste (or not), open (or not), and refined (or not). Other non-visual cues include the olfactory (such as floral perfumes which suggest modesty) and the tactile (body oils which suggest sexiness). A structuralist view of fashion assumes that stable meanings can be uncovered.

Davis (1992:91–2) argues against this position by suggesting that all consumer items—including fashionable clothes, avant-garde furniture, popular music, and objects of all kinds—have unstable meanings when they first appear on the cultural horizon. The relationship between the signifier (or word) and the signified (or thing) is arbitrary and therefore uncontrolled. Clothing items are especially ambivalent. The bra, for example, both contains and controls the breasts but also highlights them. Trousers not only conceal the male genitals but also (with the tailored fly) draw attention to them. Moreover, the meaning of consumer items is highly differentiated in terms of taste, social identity, and cultural capital. As Bourdieu (1984) has demonstrated in his empirical study of taste in French society, the function of fashion is frequently to activate these forces of differentiation. Should the relationship between the signifier and signified be weak, then the resultant 'undercoding' will produce a wide range of unanticipated interpretations and the absence of reliable knowledge. In this respect, fashion is like an aesthetic code, which is expected to be supple, and immediately able to parody, undermine, and extend the boundaries of the objects to which it refers.

The ability to differentiate fashion from the conventional clothing styles of the moment seems to rest on a flimsy, almost intuitive sense of social change. A fashionable style is one that has not yet been widely accepted. Once it is widely adopted it can lose its fashionability. Such a definition simply restates the trickle-down effect: fashion is a way of telling the time. Laver (1969a) employs this approach when describing the timetable built into fashions. Yesterday's fashions are dowdy, and those of a decade ago hideous; but with each passing decade they are seen as amusing, quaint, charming, romantic and finally (when they are old enough) categorically beautiful. When fashion, especially in appearances, is understood to be about change, then its definition rests squarely on those gestures or code modifications which 'somehow manage on first viewing to startle, captivate, offend, or otherwise engage the sensibilities of some culturally preponderant public' (Davis, 1992:15).

Take the example of blue jeans. Numerous accounts of their history exist (see Ewen and Ewen, 1982; Goldman, 1992; Lipovetsky, 1994), which itself is remarkable. The amount of scholarly attention paid to blue jeans emphasises how culturally important fashion has become. Davis's history begins in the mid-nineteenth century American west, when Morris Levi Strauss, a new immigrant from Europe, began peddling garments made from sturdy, indigo-dyed cotton said to originate in Nimes, France (hence *denim* as an anglicised pronunciation of *de Nimes*). Such a garment was also known to be worn by sailors as well as by dock workers at Genoa in Italy. Because these workers were known as 'genes' (from Genoa), the name 'jeans' became attached to the garment (Davis, 1992:69).

Jeans are now universally valued, largely because they have come to represent such glamorous attributes of western capitalism as leisure, casualness, sociability and comfort. Blue jeans herald an era of consumerism and post-industrial affluence. Intertwined with American cultural hegemony, they represent in the sociology of fashion a further instance of the power of clothing to carry a complex and symbolic content. However, a fashionable garment such as blue jeans can become so laden with different meanings that it produces only a cacophony. Both Barthes and Baudrillard have argued that fashion gravitates toward de-signification (or the destruction of meaning), because whatever meaning any fashion item may have once conveyed will be eroded by its increasing popularity. Display weakens signification, thus allowing the object to gather its own meaning and to become idiosyncratic. This explains how everyone can own a pair of blue jeans and, at the same time, derive from them a strong sense of individuality. Indeed, this is precisely what fashion does in this instance; it promises individuality through differentiation, but simultaneously amplifies the attractions of conformity. Lipovetsky describes the phenomenon of blue jeans in terms of Simmel's binary opposition between individualism and conformity: 'we can read the massive social propagation of jeans as evidence that fashion always conjugates individualism with conformity; individualism is deployed only through mimeticism' (1994:124). Fashion draws everyone towards an undefined and heartless centre. 'One dresses fashionably not so much to distinguish oneself from lower orders of society . . . [but] to be modern, to please, to express one's own individuality' (ibid.:127).

Jeans have been a remarkably successful fashion item in the light of their proliferation of styles and their wide market appeal to children, grandparents, workers, men, and women. Simultaneously, jeans can be both popular and exclusive, both inexpensive and costly designer-label garments. Jeans successfully encode status differences, and have divided the market without themselves undergoing structural change. While we may think being in fashion makes sense only by contrast with those who are not, in the case of blue jeans, much of this differentiation is hard to pinpoint; it is found in subtle, almost imperceptible signs such as the stitching along the seams, the label on the back pocket and the packaging in the retail store. Having a distinctive tag can make jeans appear original. The conspicuous label not only individuates the garment but has become part of it, like an exoskeletal building structure.

Even if fashion clothing is not strictly speaking a linguistic system, it is a mode of communication implicated in the expression of individual identity. Simmel argues that dress and other forms of fashion enable the modern urban dweller to balance the conflicting demands of social conformity with private desires for individuality. Fashion extrudes the ambivalences produced by a social self. This formulation of identity follows the precepts of social philosophers like George Herbert Mead and Charles Peirce, who assume that language is the essential socialising agent. For them, the self is produced through an inner dialogue. Fashionable dress can easily be inserted into such interior exchanges because it straddles the segregated spheres of private and public. Davis considers fashion capable of reflecting the modern, phenomenological self: 'dress, then, comes easily to serve as a kind of visual metaphor for identity and, as pertains in particular to the open societies of the West, for registering the culturally anchored ambivalences that resonate within and among identities' (1992:25).

This close association between outward appearances and a sense of self is a recurrent theme in analyses of fashion. According to Quentin Bell (1976:19), 'our clothes are too much a part of us for most of us ever to be entirely indifferent to their condition: it is as though the fabric were indeed a natural extension of the body, or even of the soul'. However, it is not just as a mirror of the self that fashion has been linked with individuality. Davis thinks clothes express our political affiliations, national identity, sexual proclivities and much more:

Were it the case, as some scholars have maintained, that fashion's sole symbolic end was registering and re-registering invidious distinctions of higher and lower, or better and lesser —that is, distinctions of class and social status—it would hardly have enough 'to talk about'; certainly not enough to account for its having thrived in Western society for as long as it has. But . . . it does have more to say: about our masculinity and femininity, our youth and age, our sexual scruples or lack thereof, our work and play, our politics, national identity and religion. (Davis, 1992:77)

As a visual metaphor, clothing is considered capable of communicating emotions. Veblen always argued that fashion expresses hostility and interclass rivalry, for conspicuous consumption readily lends itself to the demonstration of competition. Francine du Plessix Gray (1981) restates the view that fashion is a tool of envy. She recalls how Coco Chanel's wealthy clients were urged to wear cheap costume jewellery as a way of signalling disdain for *arriviste* posturing. Once the fashion caught on, however, those who owned real jewels retrieved them from bank vaults and wore them as primary symbols of social status, thus indicating the way in which fashion is used to express social contempt.

Such examples indicate how fashion can be thought of as an elaborate 'language' constituted by the subtleties of interpersonal exchange. Yet to do so is to mistake it for an actual language. More accurately, fashion is an arcane sign system, whose silent and ruthless protocols are used by some for their own purposes, such as to exclude others or exaggerate social differences. For example, when fashion is employed to display middle-class success without vulgarity, any individual who wishes to be fashionable must look rich but not *nouveau riche*. It is important to give the impression that wealth is taken for granted, that it is not an accomplishment to be flaunted. The popularity of the Ralph Lauren image in America can be explained by its success in creating an image which makes new wealth look old. It accomplished this by replacing social class insignia with the icons of an outdoor, idle lifestyle. Lauren and Polo clothes enable individuals to claim a certain status whether they have it or not. The Ralph Lauren fashion house understands fashionability in a particular way: it is about pretending not to be wealthy while dressed as if one were ready to sail yachts, play polo, ride around the cattle ranch and laze in the sun.

Bourdieu (1984) describes fashion's capacity to satisfy private aspirations as a form of cultural capital. The knowledge that taste and fashion are currencies helps the individual present a coherent social exterior, one which is capable of differentiating the chic from the tacky, in addition to preventing the exposure or betrayal of the modern, social self. Styles in clothing more often reflect than create the ambivalences they symbolise, and they can appear to bridge the gap between private desires and actual circumstances. For example, the masculinised style of dress for women in the corporate world, which became popular in the 1970s and 1980s, was constantly being feminised by soft textures such as silks and by accessorised jewellery in order to convey the message that corporate women were still women and therefore no real challenge to masculine authority. Simply to adopt a corporate style of dress is not sufficient to ameliorate the gender tensions of the workplace. After all, the actualities of business life are not so easily mediated through these symbolic transactions. Indeed, they may have very little at all to do with the character of the workplace. In the 1980s, for instance, the feminising of men's clothing—as seen in soft-shouldered and silk-textured Armani suits, floral neckties, soft leather shoes and thin, see-through socks—did not reflect any significant loss of male power in the workplace. Nor did these changes to men's appearances contribute to the rectifying of sex-based inequalities in the corporate domain.

Differences in appearances between men and women are still clear, and well illustrated with instances of underdressing and overdressing. Men can underdress on a wider variety of occasions than women. This is mainly because the serious work of men is understood to be their occupational rather than their sartorial performances. Deliberate code violations (such as mismatched socks or a foppish handkerchief) are permitted as vestmental imperfections designed to bring attention. If these 'mistakes' occur without self-consciousness, however, then their meaning is entirely different (Davis, 1992:66). The point remains that fashion can be used to express and represent desires and aspirations even though it cannot ensure their satisfaction.

Both Davis and Bourdieu want to link fashions with actual shifts in identity formations, although each acknowledges that the instabilities around gender, age and class, which are expressed and registered through different styles in clothing, are more often than not independent of their surface expressions. None the less, clothing functions as an expressive system which can be used to evoke identity without successfully defining it. Problems of status and the chronic instability of identity it engenders exist prior to any references that clothes may make to them. While fashion is often used as a 'language' in which to address these social conditions, it does not necessarily succeed in establishing or bolstering them.

The idea that fashions in dress are a mirror of their times has been championed by Quentin Bell. Seeing class differences directly reflected in clothes allows Bell to argue further that feelings, aesthetic judgements, and points of view are largely structured by class position and material circumstances. He makes the elaborate claim that fashion functions for the social sciences in the same way that the *Drosophila* (vinegar fly) has done for the scientific study of genetics. The fly is genetically mobile, constantly mutating, and yet despite its frenzied activity, it remains an invaluable scientific key to the study of genetic structures (Bell, 1976:17). Similarly fashion, in spite of its fluctuations and anomalies, is a code that unlocks the character of human society. Fashion appears to perform like a language. It is not arbitrary, but linked strategically to the ethical context constituted by the manners and codes of the moment: 'fashion . . . governs our behaviour, informs our sexual appetites, colours our erotic imagination, makes possible but also distorts our conception of history and determines our aesthetic valuations' (ibid.:62). This view is supported by others, such as Philippe Perrot (1994) in a history of nineteenth-century clothing. Perrot, however, employs the conceptual apparatus of modernity to demonstrate how, for instance, the new style of ready-made garments was a mechanism that simultaneously reflected and amplified the cultural values of conformity, regularity, and parsimony. Bell, by contrast, remains an atheoretical guide, and provides detailed descriptions of appearances only within the framework provided by Veblen, for whom fashion is an irrational system of exclusive and differentiating categories.

Analysing society through its material culture is a common approach for anthropological and historical ethnographers. But when fashion as a social process is conceived of in hyperbolic terms, as Jean Baudrillard does, then to analyse it as part of a material culture presents difficulties. Does a particular garment or style reflect values, inculcate beliefs, or express aspirations in the direct ways assumed by Lurie and Bell? Baudrillard argues that fashion does not mirror its social context, but is free-floating and unattached to any other referent than itself. Each season fashion styles pretend to refer back to themselves, to repudiate their histories, although in practice they are an effervescence of imagination. For Baudrillard, fashion in its various forms is not a relentlessly economic and market-driven force at the foundation of consumer culture, which is located in particular historical circumstances. Instead, fashion is independent and self-enclosed: it 'speculates on the recurrence of forms on the basis of their death and stockpiling, like signs, in an a-temporal reserve. Fashion cobbles together, from one year to the next, what "has been", exercising an enormous combinatory freedom' (Baudrillard, 1993:89).

A contemporary example of how fashions can be read as complex but surprisingly unrevealing—and as theoretically informed but too ambiguous to be persuasive—is supplied by Lee Wright's (1992) description of an apparently absurd fashion, namely, undersized clothes for adults. Lurie and Bell would read this fashion as a comment on the late twentieth century's cult of youth; at the same time, it seems to illustrate Baudrillard's view that fashion is an eruptive, random aesthetic. The style features a woollen jersey cropped too short to reach the waist, leggings which stop half-way up the thigh, short-legged jeans, and sloppy T-shirts with very tight arms. These garments create the impression that the body is too big, as if the body had matured while the sensibilities remained those of a child. Wright argues that the tightness and smallness of the garment accentuate the body in ways that draw attention to its gender attributes. These fashions are a sartorial 'language' which speaks of both anarchy and hierarchy. For while these garments approximate the conventional, they also challenge it: they are small but not too small; they fit but not quite; they are tight but not too tight; they cover the body but not totally (Wright, 1992:53). The mini-skirt illustrates this well, in so far as it is a miniaturisation of a 'real' size skirt, although its cropped and tight styling, by revealing both the body and undergarments, thereby undermines an ostensible function of clothing. The mini-skirt seems environmentally friendly by avoiding the wasteful use of excessive material, yet it can also appear anti-feminist, since it restricts movement just as much as stiletto heels, tight-laced corsets and hooped skirts. The apparent freedom of movement promised by the smallness of the garment is subverted by the difficulty of wearing it.

Do such interesting readings of fashion styles reveal the social milieu? Do they provide analytic tools for explaining aesthetic formations? Does fashion speak of its context, or (as Baudrillard suggests) only to itself? In our technologically sophisticated society, where images are immediate and inescapable, the significance of fashion seems dependent on its modes of expression. Since movies are a powerful advocate of fashion, fashion's communicative reach has been extended as a consequence of its appropriation by the film industry. Jane Gaines (1990) has demonstrated how costumes in classical Hollywood films functioned as narrative devices for telling women not only how to dress but also what moral forms to enact in their behaviour. Although clothing is not mapped directly on to narrative, and 'although all characters, regardless of gender, are conceived as "costumed" in motion pictures, a woman's dress and demeanor, much more than a man's, indexes psychology; if costume represents interiority, it is she who is turned inside out on screen' (Gaines, 1990:181).

The common assumption at work in these cinematic constructions of character is that there are strong connections between the inner and outer. Clothing becomes an index of cinematic character. In formula western or cowboy films, this is illustrated by the bad guys being dressed in black and the good guys in white. In dramatic films, such details as gloves, shoes, a scarf or the neckline of a dress may be used to reveal murderous intent or lack of moral integrity. Gaines (ibid.:185) reports that the early instruction manuals given to potential screenwriters drew attention to dress as an important device for developing plot and characterisation. There was an unarticulated assumption that how individuals looked, and what impressions and reactions were expressed through their mannerisms and general demeanour, were keys to the character's personality. It was thought possible to manipulate the opinions of others by self-consciously stylising one's appearance. Conversely, one could read in appearances those characteristics which were being concealed: 'not only did costume, like decor, provide iconographic cues related to typage and narrative conventions; in the absence of sound it was seen as a substitute for speech' (ibid.:188).

In both the silent and early sound films the metaphoric literalisation of costume resulted in screen figures being given flat and unchanging characters. For instance, women could be dressed as vamps, man-traps, honest simple workers or scheming sharks. Bold designs in clothes such as enlarged collars and exaggerated skirts were employed to make character statements. Later, when film types became more complex, characters acquired changeable and hidden qualities which often contributed to the narrative tension. Clothing styles were then less reliable as an index of personality.

The visual impact of fashionable goods has made them a naturalised component of cinematic representations of everyday life. Cinematic images of opulent lifestyles are easily assimilated with the promises of a consumerist social philosophy which locates social identity in the activity of buying. This triangulation of identity construction with the entertainment industries and a consumer-dominated culture coincides with the massive expansion of advertising in Hollywood. In addition to publicising brand-name products and consumer lifestyles, the cinema has helped to raise a sartorial consciousness by associating popular film stars with particular fashion styles. When stars like Elizabeth Taylor and Bette Davis wore cinematic costumes which turned up later in fashion magazines like *Vogue* and *Seventeen*, a new style of femininity was put into circulation (Turim, 1990:222). The adoption of the 'Annie Hall' look from the Woody Allen film of the same name gave women an everyday ensemble which included such masculine items as a waistcoat, necktie, flat shoes, hat and oversized pants. The style persisted for many years in the ready-to-wear fashion markets of the westernised world. As a new mode of femininity, it employed the masculine prerogatives of waistcoat and necktie without being perceived by men as threatening, since all that the appropriated look evoked was the bumbling and dishevelled characterisation of Annie Hall.

These instances of the ways in which the images produced by clothes have been literalised as instructions on how to look and conduct oneself support the general idea that fashion conveys information about behaviour. Although the fantasy world of the cinema is obviously separate from the actual conditions of everyday life, the intermingling of fashions with aesthetic injunctions about femininity and masculinity suggests that such images function mimetically. The close correspondence between women's fashions and cinematic depictions of femininity illustrates how the imagined and the imitated flow into one another. Even though fashions do not constitute a linguistic system in the technical sense, they embody a set of meanings that circulate widely in everyday life.

4

The Fashioned Self

*We must destroy here and now the widely held prejudice that
fashion is only concerned with the outer cover of man ...*

René König

Individuality seems synonymous with modernity, even though its
emergence into intellectual prominence parallels other schismatic
restructurings such as those in the economic and political spheres.
Throughout western thought, the formation of subjectivity has
provided a discourse in which to explore the links between the
biographical and the historical. Under the rubric of modernity,
the emphasis given to individualism has become constitutive of
all social practices. Fashion is implicated in these practices because
it installs in individuals their sense of being located in the present
moment. Fashion produces a social logic that informs individuals
how to think and organise their everyday life. Even though fashion
may seem a frivolity, it is highly significant in the formation of
modern consciousness. Some regard fashion as a measure of
liberality, reflecting how well people respond to change, and
how tolerant they are of difference. Fashion is not just about
categorising and ranking material culture; it is also about the
manipulation of desire, pleasure and the play of the imagination.
Simmel (1950; 1971) acknowledges this in his early essays on
fashion and body adornment. He understood fashion to be based

largely on an unresolved tension between the desire for personal distinction and the opposite desire for union with others through conformity.

Simmel's essays on fashion and adornment follow from Veblen's (1899) analysis of the leisure class in assuming that 'the fashions of the upper stratum of society are never identical with those of the lower; in fact, they are abandoned by the former as soon as the latter prepares to appropriate them' (Simmel, 1971:296). Fashion and class are assumed to be as intertwined as fashion and individuality. The binary representation of fashion—described by Simmel as a dual desire for conformity on the one hand and individual differentiation on the other—indicates that economic theories of fashion (which treat it as preoccupied with status) do not go far enough. Fashion is also about those psychological manoeuvres performed between individuals which, in many instances, express and formulate entirely modern psychological characteristics.

In his essay on adornment, Simmel elaborates the play and counterplay of appearances by suggesting that the pleasures of self-decoration are simultaneously threefold: to elicit the admiration of the other, to demonstrate superiority over the other, and to be desired and even envied by the other (see also du Plessix Gray, 1981). The individual's adorned appearance produces a radiating emanation which not only gives pleasure to onlookers, but also enhances the status of the person adorned: 'the radiations of adornment, the sensuous attention it provokes, supply the personality with . . . an enlargement or intensification of its sphere: the personality, so to speak, *is* more when it is adorned' (Simmel, 1950:340).

Metals and jewels enhance this aura or radiance in which adornment shrouds the body. Simmel literally sees the body as shinier, more mirror-like, when fashionable accessories are metallic.

> By virtue of this brilliance, its wearer appears as the center of a circle of radiation in which every close-by person, every seeing eye, is caught. As the flash of the precious stone seems to be directed at the other—like the lightning of the glance the

eye addresses to him—it carries the social meaning of jewels, the being-for-the-other, which returns to the subject as the enlargement of his own sphere of significance. The radii of this sphere mark the distance which jewelry creates between men —'I have something which you do not have'. (ibid.:343)

Simmel regards this kind of adornment as more civilised; it is less natural than tattoos and scarifications which are inscribed on the body directly and cannot be changed. Adornments, more than any garments, intensify the allure of the individual's appearance because they are usually superfluous and far removed from their origins. Jewels, metals, and precious stones are solid, autonomous and sensuous; they lack individuality. Their hardness, coldness and lack of malleability give them a style of their own, and this impersonality is the essence of their elegance. When individuals wear jewels, they themselves seem layered with another aesthetic dimension. Like furniture or utensils, jewellery is self-sufficient, and is added on to the individual as part of a 'super-contingent' value structure (ibid.). Anyone who wears such adornments is enhanced by the implication that an additional and superior capability has been extracted from the otherwise unyielding material of the ornament. 'Adornment, thus, appears as the means by which [the individual's] social power and dignity is transformed into visible, personal excellence', writes Simmel. 'Every property is an extension of personality; property is that which obeys our wills, that in which our egos express, and externally realize, themselves' (ibid.:343–4).

The fashioned body coexists with an equally fashioned self. Yet this does not close off the self as a purely psychological entity. For Simmel, fashion traverses both the psychological and social realms, and is a technique which can manufacture social cohesion. Fashionable individuals in control of their appearance signal to others a series of complex and contradictory manoeuvres. They may be expressing a desire to be recognised as a legitimate member of a specific social group; or that they are superior to other members in their social group; or that they understand themselves to be attractive and envied by subordinates outside their group. For Simmel, the power of fashion extends to the individual's manner of thinking. 'In the *adorned* body, we possess *more*', he writes, for 'if we have the adorned body at our disposal, we are masters over more and nobler things'. He therefore finds it 'deeply significant that bodily adornment becomes private property above all', since 'it expands the ego and enlarges the sphere around us which is filled with our personality' (ibid.:344).

The fashioned body speaks more eloquently, elicits more attention from others, and shrouds the individual with thicker layers of meaning and style. The adorned body reflects a more complex ego, a more visible social being who is capable of attracting the attention of others, and thereby the means for securing further self-enhancements. Fashionability emanates from the desire to control one's environment and wrest from it all that is self-promoting. Fashion provokes envy. By hijacking the opinions of others, it therefore becomes for Simmel part of everyday power relations.

Simmel can find no aesthetic or functional explanation of fashion. 'There is not a trace of expediency in the method by which fashion dictates, for example, whether wide or narrow trousers, colored or black scarfs shall be worn' (1971:297). At times fashion dictates that we wear 'ugly and repugnant' styles, and the only justification for this is as an exercise in power. Fashion represents the power to make us social: by drawing individuals away from a base nature, it inducts us all into the logics of sociality.

Simmel argues that society is possible only because the conflicting tensions between, say, a desire for the idiosyncratic and the pleasure of mutual dependence—the need to imitate, and the need to be distinguished—are fused in the individual's consciousness. Fashion is a means of accomplishing this, thus, for Simmel, it figures as a sign of progress. His view of civilisation is that the more 'natural' a society is, the more dominated it will be by customs and a sense of stability. Whereas 'primitive races' regard novelties as signs of evil, in western civilisation 'whatever is exceptional, bizarre or conspicuous, or whatever departs from the customary norm, exercises a peculiar charm upon the man of culture, entirely independent of material justification' (ibid.:300).

Fashion thus measures intellectual engagement. Societies progress from change, fashion is a form of change, the fashionable individual is constantly engaged with intellectual restructuring, so the logic is that fashion reflects not only an individual's capacity for and tolerance of change, but also a society's level of civilisation and sensitivity toward achieving progress. Simmel maintains that the more primitive a society is, the less it will change—where change is conceived of as an emanation of nervous energy. Consequently, 'the more nervous the age, the more rapidly its fashions change' (ibid.:302). The desire for change explains 'why the real seat of fashion is found among the upper classes' (ibid.), whose social location makes them restless for amusements which they have the inclination and resources to invent. Following Veblen's notion that the upper class invents fashion in order to remain exclusive, Simmel added the idea that when fashions spread from their origins they are destined for oblivion. As fashionable practices become more popular, their impact is weakened, since their popularity makes them appear natural and consequently less disruptive and less interesting. Such a view anticipates Roland Barthes' observation that 'fashion is never anything but an amnesiac substitution of the present for the past' (1985:298). For Simmel, writing fifty years before Barthes, fashion occupies the dividing line between past and future, and thereby focuses attention on the status quo and the present moment (1971:303). This concentration on the present can be a measure of how well progress is being made toward an ideal of civilisation. The justification for fashion, which Simmel provided, is sometimes echoed nowadays by those who argue that the proliferation of styles and fashions in human appearances and lifestyles indicates that we live in a liberalised, less constraining and more fluid cultural environment (see Wilson, 1985; Craik, 1994; Lipovetsky, 1994).

In a social universe of fixed hierarchies—such as a feudal order where status, class and sex are assumed to be stable categories—the role of clothing is unambiguous and limited. In contemporary westernised societies, however, fixed hierarchies no longer provide such clear depictions of order, and so clothing often functions to obscure a person's rank. Fashion becomes a masquerade. Instead of positioning individuals in a fixed social universe, it promises to fulfil their desires to perform multiple social identities.

According to Simmel, fashion in the west is inescapable. Even when individuals claim to resist its lure, they are none the less implicated in it because of the ways in which fashion insinuates itself into the modern sensibility. 'The man who consciously pays no heed to fashion accepts its form just as much as the dude does, only he embodies it in another category, the former in that of exaggeration, the latter in that of negation' (Simmel, 1971:307). The fashion-conscious individual is a 'dude'; and although Simmel uses the masculine pronoun in his descriptions of the fashionable, he maintains that women are fashion's 'staunchest adherents' (ibid.:308). This is because women are historically the subordinate sex, and as such derive greater social rewards from avoiding any instances of individualisation. Simmel believes that women are intellectually and emotionally more stable and faithful by nature, and that to compensate for their internal stolidity they are drawn more strongly to the vicissitudes of fashion. The other side of his argument is that because men are naturally less faithful and internally more changeable their attraction to and use of fashion is correspondingly weaker (ibid.:310).

Here Simmel demonstrates the playfulness of fashion as the counterplay of sociality. 'Fashion is a complex structure in which all the leading antithetical tendencies of the soul are represented in one way or another', he observes. 'Classes and individuals who demand constant change, because the rapidity of their development gives them the advantage over others, find in fashion something that keeps pace with their own soul-movements' (ibid.:317–18). Fashion is integral to the social experience and as such it is inescapable. As long as one is social, one is fashionable. The overwhelming appeal of fashion is that it answers the problem of self-positioning: 'by reason of its peculiar inner structure, fashion furnishes a departure of the individual, which is always looked upon as proper' (ibid.:313). Fashion relieves individuals of the necessity to think; it protects them with the typical and the customary. Fashion can insulate individuals from both painful reflections and a sense of isolation. It also directs individuals to act in ways which can, if practised alone, arouse unconquerable repugnance:

> as a member of a mass the individual will do many things which would have aroused unconquerable repugnance in his soul had they been suggested to him alone. It is one of the strangest social-psychological phenomena, in which this characteristic of concerted action is well exemplified, that many fashions tolerate breaches of modesty which, if suggested to the individual alone, would be angrily repudiated. But as dictates of fashion they find ready acceptance. The feeling of shame is eradicated in matters of fashion, because it represents a united action, in the same way that the feeling of responsibility is extinguished in the participants of a crime committed by a mob, each member of which, if left to himself, would shrink from violence. (ibid.:313)

The argument begins by asserting that fashion is about conformity, social obedience and collective change. The most fashionable individual is often the most studiously conventional, although this adherence to what is acceptable often comes with exaggerated aplomb, as Simmel demonstrates when describing the 'dude':

> it is characteristic of the dude that he carries the elements of a particular fashion to an extreme; when pointed shoes are in style, he wears shoes that resemble the prow of a ship; when high collars are all the rage, he wears collars that come up to his ears; when scientific lectures are fashionable, you cannot find him anywhere else . . . he leads the way, but all travel the same road . . . the leader allows himself to be led. (ibid.:305)

Fashion is not confined to garments or appearances; it is also capable of informing aesthetics, modes of conduct, and critical opinions (ibid.:321). It can denaturalise natural forms and invert social ones. This example further demonstrates how modern individuals are able to accommodate the tensions of such binary opposites as freedom and dependence (ibid.:313–14). This is the case even with supposedly natural identificatory categories such as gender. Although Simmel assumes that masculinity and femininity are natural phenomena which are expressed differentially through change and stability, he also classifies 'unnatural' forms, such as cross-dressing, as another manifestation of the natural impulse for self-decoration: 'we cannot claim that all fashion is unnatural, because the existence of fashion itself seems perfectly natural to us as social beings, yet we can say, conversely, that absolutely unnatural forms may at least for a time bear the stamp of fashion' (ibid.:322).

The circularity and inherent contradictions in Simmel's argument about such matters are not cause for his dismissal. Indeed, postmodern perspectives on sexual identity, femininity, masculinity, and fashion explicitly rework many of those contradictory impulses analysed previously by Simmel. The punk style, the New Romantics, cross-dressing, rastas and rockabillies embody fashions which have come and gone so quickly during the 1970s and 1980s that many people missed them altogether. Ideas about masculinity and femininity have changed as quickly as the garments. But the enduring message, for theorists and the fashion-conscious alike, is that both social identity and gender identity are ideological constructs. As Caroline Evans and Minna Thornton remark, 'the body can be made, through dress, to play any part it desires, as gender coding is displaced from the body on to dress' (1989:62).

In their book on women and fashion, Evans and Thornton show how being fashionable is a flirtation with being overloaded by the different expressions and styles of an incoherent feminine ideal. Such diversities can be read as a failure of that ideal. But instead of paralysing women with a deluge of contradictions, Evans and Thornton suggest that such category confusions are liberating. What they refer to as 'the alienation that is a structural condition of being female' can also enable women to manipulate better their social position. Thus, 'if fashion is one of the many costumes of the masquerade of femininity, then those costumes can be worn on the street as semiotic battledress' (ibid.:14). Fashion need not be either an entrapment, or a mechanism for further disabling and wounding the subordinate. Fashion can be all things: experimental, playful, creative as well as oppressive.

At the point where personal enjoyment, amusement and the quest for agreeable and pleasurable experiences become everyday

preoccupations, fashion is fixed as integral to modern consciousness. This conceptual shift, by which the idea of fashion elevates
novelty and variety into sources of excitement, marks the point
where fashion succeeds in renovating not only the aesthetic and
moral structures but also the general tastes and practices of its
time. Lipovetsky (1994) argues that fashion starts to influence
other modes of thinking when the balance between high and low
cultural formations begins shifting. At such times (which differ
according to historical specificities), a more epicurean perspective
on everyday life will be evident, as well as some disaffection with
the heroic values advanced by religion and feudalism.

> From that point on, personal enjoyment tended to take
> precedence over glory, agreeableness and refinement over
> grandeur, seduction over sublime exaltation, voluptuousness
> over ostentatious majesty, the decorative over the emblematic.
> The modern cult of fashion grew out of this lowering of the
> idea of grandeur and its corollary, the raising of human and
> worldly concerns to a higher dignity. (Lipovetsky, 1994:71)

The acceptance of new fashions and practices, however, is not
a foregone conclusion, since it is not simply a matter of imposing
styles and tastes on a general market. Such an easy process
would require there to be a vacuum of tastes and ideas which any
new style could quickly fill. As with the introduction of a new
aesthetic form, whether in art, architecture, or dress, the idea
itself is not sufficient to effect the change. New styles must pass
through the industrial web of the fashion industry, namely, the
technology of manufacture, mass production, cost economics,
distribution and advertising. Unless it makes sense in these terms,
a particular fashion item will not reach the market. Crucial, too, to
the success of a style nowadays is its adoption by social leaders
such as pop stars, movie actors and prominent socialites. This
situation is not dissimilar to the practices common before the
nineteenth century, when fashions in clothing were quickly
established because people of high office wore them.

Apart from such practical considerations, the dispersion of a
fashion requires a conceptual or psychological shift, as a result of
which the division between fantasy and reality appears to be

erased. Modern advertising has been crucial in the dispersal of the fashionable in so far as it gives instruction (without being dictatorial) on how pleasures can be pursued and enjoyed. Advertising neither makes tastes uniform nor prevents individuals from developing their own judgement and discernment. As Lipovetsky points out, 'advertising helps stir up desire in all its states', and 'has given rise to a broad-based fashion desire', which is a 'desire structured like fashion' (ibid.:167). In other words, advertising destabilises the practices of the everyday in order to reinvent them. In so doing, it 'stirs up desire' and thus loosens the strictures of the social order.

Advertising caters to the pleasures of looking at images and encountering the fashionable, the novel and the confusing. It can increase the volume of sales on a massive scale by directing the public to particular products, but it cannot ensure their purchase (Goldman, 1992:1–5). Advertising does not impel; it can merely invite individuals to recreate and masquerade in the manner of the proffered images. Advertising of fashionable goods can also help break down the 'opposition between fantasy as internal, unreal, private, and reality as external' (Rabine, 1994:63). When fashions are popular, they accomplish this amalgamation: the private and escapist realm of fantasy seems to collapse into the real and public domain of social practice.

Fashion magazines, with their increasing popularity and seductive appeal, seem to propel this transaction. Although ostensibly they report on the availability of goods, and introduce readers to a never-ending array of new styles, fashion magazines also evince a more didactic character. They instruct in the creation of image and self-representation. They link fantasy with self-production in ways that satisfy desires for control and novelty. As Lipovetsky remarks, 'the psychologising of appearance is accompanied by the narcissistic pleasure of transforming oneself in one's own eyes and those of others, of "changing one's skin", feeling like—and becoming—someone else, by changing the way one dresses' (1994:79).

The historian Leslie Rabine explains how the daily act of donning clothing and cosmetics is deeply implicated in the 'process of enacting the fantasies of fashion magazines upon the body'.

One of the pleasures of these everyday gestures is that they are 'erotically charged'. In addition, at a symbolic level, they ritualise a mastery of biology, that is, they make the body seem tractable. By changing the unclothed, unmade-up body into 'a self-produced coherent subject', it becomes apparent that 'the pleasures of fashion include the symbolic replay of this profoundly productive moment when subjectivity emerges' (1994:64).

But even as these pleasures are experienced, they are undercut by the impossibility of matching the ideal. To enjoy the moment when fashionable clothing and a well-groomed style give one a sense of being attractive is also to be aware of having failed to replicate the perfection displayed in the fashion photograph. The perfect image can never be achieved. Rabine (1994) argues that this failure is foundational to the continuous allure of fashion. The 'look' is always beyond, out of reach, and hence it always seems attractive. Rabine draws the psychoanalytic conclusion that fashion succeeds by promising to annul the fragmented condition of modernity with the imposition of a coherent subjectivity.

The logic of this position is that the contemporary woman interested in fashion is expected to become a self-reflecting subject. She is required to think about and to know how she is being looked at, as well as how her status as an object to be pleasurably gazed upon has been formulated. Yet there is an inherent contradiction in all of this; at the very moment when women are depicted as self-producing, what they are constructing is the constrained and subjugated image of the heterosexually desirable female. 'The more she is portrayed as independent, the more she is portrayed as an object of the male look. The woman of fashion is invited to assume custodianship of that look, and to find her own empowerment through managing the power that inevitably reduces her to the second sex' (Rabine, 1994:65).

Rabine's analysis of fashion magazines between the 1960s and 1980s uncovers a persistent dualism in classifications of femininity. On the one hand, women are given images of themselves as confident, free, and sexually powerful individuals who can display these qualities through their skilful use of clothing and cosmetics. On the other hand, during the last two decades, these same fashion magazines have published reports of women's submission and vulnerability, with articles on domestic violence, increasing rape rates, salary inequalities, sexual harassment in the workplace, and other events and practices which demonstrate that women are merely objects in a man's world (ibid.:66). The upshot is that fashion magazines pedal a bifurcated subjectivity for women, which combines the contrary illusion of an exuberant and self-possessed femininity with the expectation of being vulnerable to the power exercised in male-dominated economic and political spheres. Rabine's point is not that these images are contradictory and confusing, but that they succeed in shaping female subjectivity in a way that naturalises the ambivalent social position of contemporary women, whose situation is thus even more dire than being simply seduced by the fashion system. Theoretically, situations can be imagined in which women escape this trap. But in Rabine's analysis, where women internalise both their power and lack of it, no other position is possible. Modern women simply oscillate between perfect femininity as sexual power, and perfect femininity as object of male pleasure.

Although fashion seems gender-biased in its obsession with femininity and the female image, men are not beyond its orbit. In the late twentieth century, men's austere appearances are undergoing a second major renovation. The first coincided with the bourgeois revolution and marked the relinquishing of male visibility. Men began to contain their narcissistic and exhibitionist desires and gave up wearing the sumptuous and flamboyant dress of the aristocracy. The corresponding uniformity in masculine attire helped conceal class distinctions. Irrespective of his social position, if a man were employed in a service, professional or technical capacity, he would wear a business or lounge suit. When attending public ceremonies, he would be similarly dressed. It took a trained and highly critical eye to observe the class distinctions between a man's suit individually tailored on Savile Row and a mass-manufactured, off-the-rack uniform.

The new masculine style of plain tailoring and block colours has become the requisite costume of the white-collar urban worker, and reflects his dependable and hard-working social position. As the dress of someone who can confidently ask for someone else's money or power, it is the required look of bankers, merchants and professional politicians. Such uniformity, however, is not ideal because the demonstration of wealth still remains important to displays of masculinity. Men thus recruit their wives and children to display success, as Veblen noted in the case of the nineteenth-century bourgeois and upper-class woman, whose exemption from labour enabled her to consume vicariously on behalf of the male head of the household.

In the psychic economy described by psychoanalysis, the impulses toward exhibitionism and narcissism are not simply overcome but redirected. J. C. Flügel argues that men now assert their social visibility through three mechanisms: professional performance or 'showing off'; scopophilia (or voyeurism), and the related identification with woman-as-spectacle in a variety of instances, ranging from shopping to fetishism and transvestism. In other words, men have displaced their own bodily narcissism, exhibitionism, and pleasure in luxury and ornamentation on to women.

The public body, whether it is female or male, is always mediated through vestimentary codes. Styles of clothing shape what we see when looking at the 'natural' body. Clothing and fashionability become features of subjectivity when the surface of the body is imagined through styles in dress. Working from a psychoanalytic interpretation of fashion, Silverman (1986) makes the point that gender differences have become more visible during the last century and are represented in gender-specific dress styles. Men's wear, in particular, has solidified into a uniform sobriety and rectitude, whereas by contrast women's styles have fluctuated rapidly, thus creating the impression of female flighti-ness. The few attempts at bridging these differences, such as women wearing neckties and business suits, do not challenge Silverman's argument, but merely demonstrate again both the instability and eclecticism of the feminine in matters of dress.

Such emphasis on the subjectivity of appearance does not occlude the recognition of fashion as a socio-economic phenom-enon. On the contrary, it adds to our understanding that 'clothing not only draws the body so that it can be seen, but also maps out the shape of the ego, [such that] every transformation within a society's vestimentary code implies some kind of shift within its ways of articulating subjectivity' (Silverman, 1986:149). Even though male and female styles in clothing have merged in recent decades, gender differences have not been submerged. Lipovetsky (1994:109) describes how such differentiation is now much more subtle, and requires a correspondingly closer reading of 'little nothings'—the woman's necktie made of different material from a man's, her shirt tailored with 'feminine' buttons, and the belt buckle gendered into male and female versions.

As women have become more active in the public domain, they have partially abandoned their position as emissaries for men, and begun to use fashion and appearance for their own self-expression. In this reappropriation of an already existing system of social classification, new configurations in meaning have come into play. These have not sparked the kind of category crisis that cross-dressing brings about, but they certainly signal not only a permeability at the boundaries but also the possibility of disruptions provoked by the designation of the category itself (see Garber, 1992). Styles of appearance are public claims for inclusion within a category, and whenever these styles are toyed with, then fashion is reiterating its ability to influence human subjectivity. Fashion is here in service to the ethic of individualism. How individuals choose to look, how they want others to see them, designates the fashioned body as a site for acting out a variety of social claims. Fashioning the body becomes a practice through which the individual can fashion a self.

5

Gender Shopping

It was Woman the shops were wrangling over in rivalry, it was Woman they caught in the everlasting snare of their bargains, after they had dazed her with their displays. They had awoken new desires in her weak flesh, they were an immense temptation to which she inevitably yielded . . .

Émile Zola

In the late nineteenth century, medical tracts were written about an apparent epidemic associated with those department stores from which women stole indiscriminately, without need or reason. At the height of the epidemic in 1896, kleptomania was officially reported at the rate of a thousand cases a year, but unofficial figures doubled the number (Camhi, 1993:29). The department store played a critical role in the distinctions made between pathological and criminal forms of kleptomania. Pathological kleptomania was thought to be provoked by the department store: its abundant displays of exotic and sensuous goods, its disorienting floor plan, and its democratisation of luxury all conspired to induce moral lassitude in women, who were silently urged to take possession of whatever appealed to them. These desires, often in conjunction with inherently 'female' weaknesses such as hysteria, feeble-mindedness, and neurasthenia, erupted into acts of kleptomania. The medical diagnoses of the time often linked kleptomania with critical stages during the menstrual cycle. Older women, for instance, would steal to compensate for the uterine losses of menopause (ibid.:30).

Women were also thought to become kleptomaniac through imitation, which, pertinently, happened to be the same mechanism that induced them to be fashionable. The very style of women's clothing, their large skirts and layered garments, facilitated theft by enabling them to conceal stolen booty on their persons. In the nineteenth-century novel, *Ladies' Delight* (1883), Émile Zola describes the workings of the new department store, basing his account closely on the *Bon Marché*, which was opened by Aristide Boucicaut in Paris in the early 1850s. Zola's fictional store, *Au Bonheur des Dames*, is described as a 'modern cathedral', and is a home to the new religion of consumerism. The novel details the beginnings of this bourgeois cultivation of material desires, and the retail practices that shaped the psychological characteristics of shoppers and employees alike. Zola shows how the store created a sexual divide between female shoppers and male retailers, and how the power of fashion was used to compel women to act against their better interests sometimes to the point of developing those pathological behaviour patterns later known as kleptomania. Deliberate tactics employed in such stores seduced customers into buying more than they could afford, desiring objects that were useless. They also tempted shoppers with opportunities for stealing.

Michael Miller's (1981) historical analysis of the nineteenth-century Parisian department store demonstrates how a climate of moral vertigo was deliberately created in order to disorient, dazzle and confuse customers. Conventional moral restraints were thus destabilised and replaced by an ethos of unrestrained desire. Kleptomania was a symptom of the moral laxity produced by the stores' displays of luxury. In the early department store, the world of objects and the constituents of subjectivity were interwoven promiscuously. According to Bowlby (1985), the new department store was the site of a new sexual order. Women and men interacted differently in this 'temple to Woman': femininity was associated with consumerism, and masculinity with money-making. The twin secular impulses of modernity, sex and money, were blended together in the department store, where new configurations of human emotions were being styled. Among Zola's characters, Madame de Boves succumbs to the new mental disorder of kleptomania, and Madame Marty, who was once a modest and quiet housewife, becomes a compulsive shopper. Consumerism is contagious and individuals become its victims. The art of selling is really the art of deception; the display of goods creates confusion between illusions and reality. Zola describes how display dummies came to look like real women (and vice versa) in a gesture which implied that shoppers are objects—and like all objects—can be bought and sold:

> The dummies' round bosoms swelled out the material, their ample hips exaggerated the narrowness of the waists, their missing heads were replaced by large tickets with pins stuck through them into the red bunting in the necks; while mirrors on either side of the windows, by a deliberate trick, reflected and multiplied them endlessly, populated the street with these beautiful women who were for sale, and who bore their prices in large figures, in the place of their heads. (Zola, 1883:10)

These department stores housed feminine desires in much the same way that museums housed masculine achievements. In the department store, a woman was shown goods which held out the tacit promise of inciting men's desire for her. The department store became the site of an unruly feminine impulse to consume; Gillian Swanson describes nineteenth-century female shoppers as becoming 'drunk with the glitter' (1994). The female narcissism which compelled women to shop could also disrupt the public arena. Department stores helped curb these impulses by locating the desire for the feminine in purchasable goods. In this way, consumer goods were linked with expressions of sexuality. The purchase of objects then became an end in itself, and femininity turned out to be just another consumer good. In the department store, a woman could learn to be feminine; she was given the opportunity to enact herself before an audience of shoppers and retailers, both women and men.

When femininity is conceptualised as a performance or masquerade, it is readily appropriated by the psychoanalytic tradition which fuses fashion, femininity and fetishism into elegant diagnoses of pathology. Camhi (1993:39–43) cites the work of an early twentieth-century French psychiatrist who describes women's erotic passion for fabrics (and especially silk) as a form of addiction. The reported case studies of deregulated and obsessive desire in women make use of misogynist and idiosyncratic distinctions between women and men. For instance, a silk fetishist comes off worse than a fur fetishist because the former (more often a woman) is satisfied with the feel of the fabric being pulled across and gliding over the back of the hand, whereas the latter (more often a man) finds pleasure in the stroking of the fur with the palm, which also gives sensations of resistance when brushing against the pelt. Although these highly idiosyncratic distinctions between the erotic responses of women and men to different fabrics are negligible, they were sufficient, at the turn of the century, to classify one act as pathological and the other appropriately masculine. Femininity is commonly linked to fabrics in psychoanalytic writings. In a passage by Freud, which Camhi finds strange, the connections are spelled out:

> women have made few contributions to the discoveries and inventions in the history of civilisation; there is, however, one technique which they may have invented—that of plaiting and weaving. If that is so, we should be tempted to guess the unconscious motive for the achievement. Nature herself would seem to have given the model which this achievement imitates by causing the growth at maturity of the pubic hair that conceals the genitals. (Freud, 1933, cited in Camhi, 1993:29)

It is the shame of lacking a penis which has drawn women to the use of fabrics, clothing and fashion, originally to conceal this lack, and afterwards as substitutes for it. The fashionable woman, then, approximates the dignity of any normal man by being attired in the best, most envied and respected suit of clothes. Her appearance is hysterically equivalent to masculine normalcy. Camhi rereads this passage as revealing Freud's own fear of women; 'the mythic veil of shame that Freud would have had women draw across their bodies was a tissue of his own weaving, drawn to protect him from their difference' (ibid.:29).

Before the nineteenth century, upper-class men and women were equally ornamental in their dress (Laver, 1937). Both wore excessive amounts of lace, perfume, highly coloured silks and brocades. The dramatic division between male and female appearances, which began with the emergence of the bourgeoisie, is often accounted for by industrialism, capitalism and the segregation of private from public domains. The economic and structural transformation of Europe, brought about by the bourgeois revolution, changed the appearances of men by requiring them to have an increasingly sombre dress. The new work ethic, embodied in the fashion change which Flügel (1930) calls the Great Masculine Renunciation, was a visual display designed to repudiate the aristocratic elegance, opulence and leisure which had corrupted these classes before the nineteenth century.

Flügel also argues that fashion is propelled by the shifting eroticisation of body zones. The tensions between modesty and display—said to exist as fundamental ambivalences in the individual psyche—intensify the sexualisation of appearance. Although Flügel does not discount socio-cultural forces such as class rivalries, the primary impetus of fashion stems, according to him, from the eroticising of body parts. It does not weaken his position to acknowledge that different cultures eroticise different body parts, such as the feet, lips, legs, ear-lobes, or neck. Nor is his argument damaged when various body parts shift in their erotic value within the same culture. In the west, for instance, women's buttocks, breasts and legs have been variously the focus of erotic attention, as have men's hair, chests and shoulders. For the early psychoanalysts, an impulse towards erogenous vestments was part of the human condition, and any evidence of different rates of shifting interest in the eroticised elements of dress could not undermine its universality (Bergler, 1987).

Steele (1985) continues the psychoanalytic tradition by regarding the history of fashion as an amplification of the sexual; appearances and the erotic are always inextricably linked. Fashion can induce erotic stimulation indirectly by manipulating the gaze in order to develop pleasure in looking and to teach us how to appropriate the other for our own delight. Fashion works for the individual as a way of advertising the self; it mediates between what one desires and what can be presented as socially acceptable to the other. Physically constraining fashions such as tight-lacing and stiletto-heeled shoes might appear to signify women's inferior position and sexual enslavement, but Steele maintains that a woman's voluntary adoption of such fashions indicates her capacity to imbue them with an eroticised sense of herself. The presented self is always an eroticised self.

Steele does not take into account the historical and economic conditions of the fashion industries. Despite an explicit focus on women and fashion, she ignores the history of women's participation in these industries as lowly employees and overlooked designers. She concentrates on fashion clothing only as an aesthetic and erotic phenomenon. Like Anne Hollander (1980), Steele thinks that clothes sexualise the body, and does not consider the antithetical possibility that it is the body which imbues clothes and outward appearances with sexuality. There are certain garments which produce highly specific sexual messages; for instance, women's shoes. These she reads in the same manner that Lurie (1992:242–3) reads handbags and purses (large, open tote bags signify a casual approach to sex; hard, closed, shiny, compact handbags symbolise a closely regimented or repressed sexuality). Steele maintains that sling-back shoes signify *décolletage*, oxfords suggest non-sexual seriousness, low-cut uppers replicate breast cleavage, open toes reveal a desire for lingerie display, and stiletto heels are a request for kinky sex.

It is easy to exaggerate the specific messages drawn from items of clothing. Some of these claims are made to amuse and to bolster a popular interest in fashion. None the less, such comments re-emphasise the sexualisation of clothing, and are reminders that styles of appearance are sexually coded. Feminist readings of fashion have often portrayed it as a kind of conspiracy to distract women from the real affairs of society, namely economics and politics. Fashion has been seen as a device for confining women to an inferior social order, largely because it demands an unequal expenditure of time and money by women on activities which do not attract the professional attention and efforts of men. Fashion works to intensify self-absorption and thereby reduces the social, cultural and intellectual horizons of women. Fashion eroticises many more aspects of women's lives than of men's; it makes women slavishly attentive to details and adds to the anxieties of their daily existence by emphasising such impossible goals as everlasting youth, slenderness, sexuality and eroticism. In short, the analysis of fashionable dress as hostile to women echoes conventional analyses of capitalism which see it as a form of women's oppression (Hansen and Reed, 1986). Fashion is part of the ruling discourse which maintains the inequalities of the status quo in a patriarchal society.

On the other hand, women's fashions have provided a great deal of freedom from certain nineteenth-century styles. The twentieth-century popularity of trousers, shirts, and different shapes in shoes has given women much more physical freedom and choice in self-representation. It can be argued that women are even freer than men to employ clothing as a social device which serves their self-interests. David Kunzle (1982), in his history of tight-lacing and corsets, has argued that nineteenth-century fashions were not so unambiguously restrictive as is often thought. He argues that body-sculpting was sexually enhancing. Against the feminist criticism that tight-lacing was ruinous to health (Roberts, 1977; Finch, 1991), Kunzle emphasises that it was not solely a form of restriction or containment. The highly sculptured look served the dual purpose of making the body appear demure while at the same time highlighting and eroticising different parts of it.

Kaja Silverman (1986) adds to this interpretation of fashion by reading the pleasures of voyeurism and exhibitionism in the culturally visible body. Dress, once the signifier of class, is now implicated more fully in the representation of gender, and particularly in the management of tensions between the masculine and the feminine. Silverman points out that not all fashions are the agents of female subjugation by a controlling male gaze. Before industrialism, the function of elegant and extravagantly ornate dress was to mark male visibility and class prerogative rather than to confine women to a secondary status. Subsequent shifts in the meaning of fashion paralleled other social changes, such as the association of wealth with industry rather than leisure. Without explicitly acknowledging the legacy of Veblen and

Simmel, Silverman understands that those changes resituated women in ways that made them social appendages emblematic of male wealth. Women were transformed into fashion slaves unable to pay for their obsession, while men abandoned the world of fashion but retained financial control over it (Silverman, 1986:139–40).

A similar point is made by Lipovetsky (1994:109): 'the representation of gender difference is proving much sturdier than the representation of social class'. An increasing number of examples demonstrates similarities in the ways men and women dress. Although men's clothing has become gradually less austere, and women's dress now shows signs of masculine origin, such developments do not indicate a disappearance of gender-linked fashions. Indeed, there remain fixed and stable styles—frozen into what Silverman calls a phallic rigidity—which female dress can adopt as a way of contesting those culturally-based power structures which women have not yet succeeded in appropriating. When women don business suits, or tuxedos as evening wear, they appear to imitate male attire but only in a way that mirrors and preserves the binary structures that separate masculine from feminine fashion. 'While women are turning in vast numbers to masculine clothing styles and men are reappropriating their right to a certain level of fantasy in dress, new distinctions are arising that reconstitute the cultural cleavage in the realm of appearance' (ibid.). Lipovetsky proceeds to point out that

> men and women alike wear pants, but the cuts and often the colours are different; shoes have nothing in common; a woman's shirt is easy to tell from a man's; the shapes of bathing suits differ, and so do those of underwear, belts, pocketbooks, watches and umbrellas. More or less everywhere, fashion articles reinscribe difference in appearance by way of 'little nothings'. (ibid.)

Fashionability can involve highly sensualised experiences. The feel of fabric can evoke private pleasures. Being clothed in a desirable ensemble can feed the individual's fantasies of developing an *alter ego*. The look of fashion, particularly the fashion photograph, rather than the fashion item itself, can provide those pleasures which impinge on the formation of identity. For Diana Fuss (1992), it is the ubiquity of fashion photography that is significant because it functions as a mechanism of cultural self-fashioning. For the huge numbers of people who look at magazines and advertisements, a sense of identity can be called into existence by the interpellation of a fashioned image. Fuss argues that when individual identity is understood to be constituted through identificatory experiences, then the interest individuals show in the fleeting parade of fashioned images can have long-term consequences on how they understand and position themselves in the world. When a heterosexual woman gazes at magazine images of her imagined and other self, these images simultaneously train her to look at other women as if she were a lesbian. Fuss notes with amusement that in this instance the identificatory mechanism has become a vehicle of contradictory and unanticipated instruction.

Fashion photography and the cinema assume a heterosexual viewer, but the perspective offered through both these media eroticise images of the female body, and encourage women to gaze at other women with that 'homospectatorial look'. 'The entire fashion industry operates as one of the few institutionalised spaces where women can look at other women with cultural impunity', Fuss writes. 'Women are encouraged to *consume*, in voyeuristic if not vampiristic fashion, the images of other women.' Consequently, 'to look straight *at* women, it appears, straight women must look *as* lesbians' (Fuss, 1992:713).

Fuss argues that fashion photography situates the viewer in ways that awaken the unconscious homosexual desire once played out through the mother–daughter bond. Fashion promises repossession of the lost face, smile, gaze, touch, smell of the maternal. Additionally, as fashion photography commonly presents images that dismember the female body into fetishised parts—lips, smile, breasts, eyebrows, face—female subjectivity becomes attached to overvalued zones of the body: 'the *promise* these photographic images hold of reconnecting (re-fusing?) the homosexual–maternal relation, goes a long way toward explaining the enduring fascination that fashion photography holds for its female viewers, the pleasures it seeks to provide, as well as the discomforts it may inadvertently summon' (ibid.:735).

A similar point is made by Neil Spencer (1992) in his analysis of recent male fashion images in the popular magazines *GQ*, *Esquire* and *Arena*. These images rework men as sensitive, willing to assume paternal responsibilities and ready to defer to women without a sense of being personally threatened. Feminism may well have influenced this refashioning, yet Spencer points out that this observation is misleading. The men depicted in these fashion images are still more interested in themselves than they are in women. The new man is just less covert about such matters: 'it is one of the ironies of the male press that while outvying each other in red-blooded heterosexuality, and murmuring asides to their female readers, their substantial gay readership is addressed only through homoerotic fashion plates' (Spencer, 1992:44).

To identify people as either male or female is often assumed to be the first step in human sociality. When these categories are not well established, when the expected characteristics of gender are either not visible or appear ambiguous, then the social act becomes problematic. The expected manners and codes of conduct in the social exchange are suddenly unavailable, and individuals become unsure how to speak, what to say, how to position their bodies, and how to respond to the other. In every human society, appearances are policed. Those categories of gender which seem to underwrite heterosexuality are seen more properly as one of the rhetorical effects it produces. Representations of gender are deeply inserted into the vernacular of the modern. The taken-for-granted mannerisms and behaviour patterns of the everyday clearly designate gender. If these signs fail, or there is some degree of ambiguity in appearance—if the woman appears moustached, or the man appears to have breasts—then the momentum of social exchange is destabilised. The physical signs that suggest androgyny or ambiguity are not merely overlooked as anomalous but instead become points of social chaos.

In her study of transvestism, Marjorie Garber (1992) gives an account of how female-to-male cross-dressers can learn some useful tricks by taking advice from John T. Molloy's best-selling books, *Dress for Success* (1975) and *The Woman's Dress for Success*

Book (1977). Molloy assumes that in the competitive, corporate world, dress can make a great deal of difference to the individual's upward mobility. He details numerous instances of disadvantageous dress styles such as the 'imitation man look', which shows how women lose their authority when they wear a pin-striped suit, shirt, tie and felt hat. Molloy's advice to the small man on how to use the insignia of authoritative male dress has been appropriated as equally valuable, Garber points out (1992:44–5), to the diminutive female cross-over. To avoid looking cute, like a small boy in man's clothing, Molloy advises ultra-traditional styles—a white shirt, a serious tie in the Ivy League tradition, wing-tip shoes, and luxurious fabrics like fine wool and cashmere. The rules of conventional appearance are here appropriated for the purposes of masquerade. When fashion is deliberately enlisted to enhance appearance, the result is very often a convincing performance.

In contemporary society, a frequent complaint is that men are left out of the fashion rush. This objection could not have been made in Regency England when the dandy Beau Brummell came to political prominence, not because of his aristocratic pedigree but on account of his immaculate linen and new style of dressing (Moers, 1960). But in the late twentieth century, it can seem as if men have become fashion *habitués* only recently. The arrival of non-corporate styles, such as casual wear, particularly, blue jeans, boat shoes, leather jackets and logo-smothered sports apparel, have made them fashion targets.

The styles now available to men include the new Italian macho look of expensive Armani suits, the urban cowboy and the retro rockabilly. Sean Nixon (1992) insists that these options indicate a broadening of men's identity roles. He supports his point by referring to the physical layout of men's clothing stores. The displays in these settings constitute a narrative which draws the individual shopper into a plausible rehearsal of his own social aspirations. The shop may have only a few items of clothing on display, but as the shopper follows a deliberate floor plan, he encounters items of clothing arranged to construct a sense of different lifestyles and their associated sensibilities. There may be old cricket bats, canoe paddles and dark, wooden-framed mirrors, which evoke a sense of the landed gentry, and then a professional business suit, attaché case and city paraphernalia such as umbrellas and neckties to indicate a more metropolitan look. Or the shop floor may be crowded with possibilities, including the urban cowboy look, the casual suburban look and the ambitious city look. The suggestions being made cannot all be focused on the one individual; there are more identities available than opportunities to live them out. The point is that various narratives of masculine identity are nowadays on display (see also Reekie, 1992).

Nixon notes that there is a more aggressive mixing up of the conventional signifiers of masculine appearance, and even the occasional parodying of them: 'motorcycle boots are worn with trunks or lacy boxers, topped off with tank-top and jacket; or else, Doc Marten boots mix with jumper and trunks replete with knuckleduster' (1992:162). These are some of the images appearing in the avant-garde fashion magazines. And just as women's fashion magazines contain extreme versions of everyday feminine garb, so the male-oriented magazines are following suit. In both instances, the social function is much the same—the spectacularising of gender identities.

The historian Gail Reekie, however, does not take this proliferation of gender images to be a sign of their merging or weakening. Indeed, she maintains that although sexual identities are unambiguous, gender insignia have become unclear in the market-place:

> sexual identities remain firmly fixed within contemporary culture, despite the efforts of the marketing industry to encourage consumers to ignore the constraints of conventional repertoires. The meanings, formulations and associations of masculinity and femininity are, however, subject historically to transformation, subversion, dis-connection and re-connection. The sexual meanings associated with the clearly delineated spaces of the department store have in some instances become disaggregated and dispersed. The sexual message that emerged so clearly from the department store has become garbled. (Reekie, 1992:188)

From her historical analysis of the new-style shopping mall, Reekie observes that the greater involvement of men as fashion buyers has altered the status of consumption. Shopping has been elevated from a form of drudgery into a source of entertainment and pleasure. In her example of the development of a local shopping mall, Reekie points out that its physical proximity to a proposed sex-leisure centre (containing peep-shows, stage acts and a 'love hotel' catering for men) changes the rhetorical appeal of shopping. The culture of consumption, which has previously catered to the feminine, may begin to disadvantage women and favour men. 'Women shoppers of the 1990s can no longer assume that shopping sites will offer sanctuary from male culture' (ibid.:191). Whereas once it was unmanly to shop, now, Reekie points out, 'it is possible for a man to simultaneously engage in consumer behaviour and maintain his masculine identity' (ibid.:192).

Fashion photography has also contributed to the framing of a new masculinity, not so much by emphasising new styles in clothing, but by emphasising the male physique and attributing to men certain natural qualities often characteristic of women, namely submissiveness and passivity. 'Shifting patterns of consumption and the proliferation of gay and feminist social critiques paved the way for the emergence of the "new man"' (Triggs, 1992:25). When the male model in the Levis laundrette advertisement removes his jeans, presumably to wash them, the image suggests that in so doing, he is appropriating the 'female' domain of the laundry for his own pleasures (ibid.:26). The sulking, pouting facial expressions and submissive body positions adopted in this advertisement graft on to men many of the stereotypical female qualities associated with a more 'primitive' (that is, emotional) nature.

Women have often been intimately linked with fashionable goods, as if the latter's frivolousness were enough to explain women's obsession. Fashion photography and journalism have been instrumental in forging this relationship, particularly in the twentieth century. Cathy Griggers's (1990) study of how the fashion industry depicts women rightly questions the legitimacy of this linkage. Even though twentieth-century fashion has focused more directly on women, it does not necessarily follow that women are more attuned to it than men. Nor is it adequate to explain the connection in terms of economic exploitation, and to argue that women's secondary social status makes them more vulnerable to the dominant order. According to Griggers, the institutions of fashion, the mass media and advertising are all deeply implicated in the discursive formation of women's identities. These industries have appropriated the Freudian question, 'what do women want?' and answered it in self-serving terms: 'she wants everything' (1990:96). However, Griggers interrogates that position and argues that the mechanism of desire which operates in the fashion system draws into its orbit not just women but every consumer, irrespective of gender or age.

In our contemporary consumer society, women's identities have been fractured, divided, redivided and newly created in order to multiply the opportunities and niche markets for fashion-driven products. The fashion industries have thrived on the instability of women's identity, and have continued to burden women with the putative need to reinvent themselves constantly. Women are ubiquitously portrayed in various and often contradictory poses as 'the "new" woman, the working woman, the sports woman, the family woman, the sexually liberated and educated woman' (ibid.). This chameleon is capable of looking attractive in 'high-impact shades, reptile gloves, evening gowns by Ungaro, spiked heels, and a divided skirt'. In addition, she is to be found in every conceivable setting:

> we find her in a dream interior, a corridor leading nowhere in particular, a concrete landscape, a menacing metropolis. We find her in the bedrooms and gardens of the rich, or hiding in the nostalgia of a former century's elegance, lying in abandoned rooms ... [She is] fetish bearer, identificatory dare, social ideal, object of desire, desiring subject, art work, commodity object, mother, power dresser, consumer, mannequin—fashion itself. She seems sometimes bedazzled, sometimes bold, sometimes just plain bored and waiting. (ibid.:77)

This constant rearticulation of the feminine is the perennial concern of the fashion industries, and becomes the daily concern of consumers. This is how a commodity-dominated culture is sustained: by investing cultural meaning in objects, real and imagined, within an open-ended economy of signs. For example, a garment widely pictured in department stores, fashion magazines and the mass media, which has an exorbitant price-tag attached to it, may be beyond the purchasing power of most consumers. None the less, it can still function as an element in the identificatory process because the idea of possessing it provides the individual with a sense of the sexual and social power it signifies. Desire thus brings what is materially out of reach within imaginative reach.

The visual and cultural tensions that attach to desired and fashionable objects are replayed in the individual's own social world. Objects which have no human qualities—such as cars, clothes and cosmetics—become gendered and visibly sexualised. These desired objects are not necessary components of normative reality; on the contrary, their social value as codes in any individual's world can fluctuate wildly. Yet these fashionable items constitute a discourse of signs that is continuously shifting, and from which each of us draws together meanings and memories of other places and other times. In this respect, the codes themselves become cultural referents, and impinge on those processes which structure the self. In these ways, fashion, far from being a frivolity, is capable of reappropriating and rearticulating subjectivity, and by so doing it functions as an identificatory mechanism.

Griggers's views coincide with Jameson's and Baudrillard's theories of the self in its schizophrenic and ephemeral state yet, in a subtle reworking of the idea of the postmodern self, Griggers points out that modern women have long experienced the instability of the feminine. 'The loss of the cultural referent anchoring a normalized feminine subject . . . *is* her history' (ibid.:86). No modern woman expects to discover a stable identity in the images found in fashion journalism. Indeed, this does not work as an explanation of the fashion images' appeal.

The average reader of VOGUE participates in a discursive game which trembles between fantasy and its failure, but not only in relation to the fashion garments . . . but in relation to the cultural construction of feminine subjectivity, and its splittings, which the fashion discourse articulates. (ibid.:87)

The pleasure for women in looking at their multifarious images is the recognition that their feminine identity has always been elusive and somewhere else; men are finally recognising that their own dream of a self-empowered subjectivity is better conceived of as merely an ideological ruse. The stability of a social identity, whether masculine or feminine, is now more widely recognised as a myth. But the constant display of desirables, which the consumer society daily creates, provides the objects with which both men and women can extract satisfaction (however temporary and fleeting) for their unrestrained and fluid desires.

The relationship between subjectivity and commodity signs is enunciated through those acceptable cultural practices, such as fashion, which every social order provides. Human needs become irrelevant in a consumer-dominated culture. It is not a matter of whether we need *haute couture* or street-style clothing in order to consolidate a sense of identity, or whether these needs are manufactured to serve the interests of capitalist enterprise. The point has much more to do with how everyday social activities proceed. Fashion is a mode of social exchange, and, like other social discourses, its function is ultimately to maintain cultural continuity. The sociation, including the discourse, practices and values, around fashion does not necessarily exploit or demean individuals just because it provides neither stability nor closure; on the contrary, a benefit of the fashion system is to offer a discourse of signs and codes through which desires and subjectivities can be enunciated. As Baudrillard observes, 'objects, and the needs that they imply, exist precisely in order to resolve the anguish of not knowing what one wants' (quoted in ibid.:100).

6

The Look of Fashion

Aren't we mad to let them move us about, push us around, wrap us up, reproduce us so we are all the same or nearly so . . . I wonder if it is you or I who dictate fashion.

Sonia Rykiel

When Hélène Cixous (1994) describes her favourite evening jacket, a black, soft woollen garment designed by the illustrious Sonia Rykiel, she vividly illustrates how fashion, as a technology, can order and define the lived milieu. Cixous's elaborate meditation on this elegant, expensive, and shimmering garment depicts fashion as more than an object; it is a sensibility which pervades all aspects of everyday life and constitutes one's aesthetic inclinations. Whenever Cixous puts on her jacket, she becomes the starry night, the East, the foreign. Fashion transforms her, and she is infatuated with its capacity to do so. Fashion is not just a vestimentary overlay, a disguise of fabric and style which covers and thus rewrites and reshapes the body. Instead, it is a new way of speaking the body, and freeing it from silence. Cixous describes how the garment sometimes inhabits her as if it were a primitive deity (1994:95). It links an interior and oriental exoticism with an ancient self-knowledge that touches 'the body hidden in the body' (ibid.:96). For Cixous, the garment is continuous with her body, and not a form of armour protecting it. Her clothing 'doesn't declare its boundaries, doesn't gather in its frontiers' (ibid.). It becomes a form of cultural expression, much like writing, which renders the interior exterior. The fashion garment makes the 'inside' the 'right side': 'there is continuity between world, body, hand, garment' (ibid.:95).

Cixous regards Rykiel's fashion garments as forms of self-expression. Although she recognises that clothes can be barriers (an argument considered below, pp. 73–5) she does not share this view; 'there are shield-clothes, mirror-clothes, shimmering, dazzling clothes, clothes which both attract and repel the gaze, clothes of the armour species, clothes which remold the body to a precise measure, to perfect composure, clothes which adorn' (ibid.:97). But these are not the clothes she favours. Cixous's clothes must become part of her: by expressing her self, they will even come to resemble her. In this way, a woman's identity fuses with her appearance to become greater than the parts. Cixous denaturalises the body by making it synonymous with history and culture, and naturalises fashion by making the garment part of individual consciousness, memory and sensation.

When a body is clothed in garments that rearrange or restyle it, Cixous imagines that a tension or resistance is exuded like a sensation of friction between the skin and the fabric. The body should not be forced by its clothing. Both Cixous and Rykiel oppose the idea that clothes rearrange or reshape the individual, believing instead that body and garment should flow into each other to create that new layer of meaning or new entity which is the fashioned self. For the designer Sonia Rykiel, fashion is an extension of human creativity and imagination; in its seams and folds, a garment, like memory, records a specific sensibility. Rykiel describes how the urgency and speed of today's fashions can be misleading: 'fashion, like history, parades, all lights turned on it. It spangles and glitters . . . it sparkles from head to foot, bursting out triumphantly, gloriously, luxuriously' (Rykiel, 1994:102–3). Yet despite the attention given to it, and despite its flashiness and apparent inconstancy, fashion is a durable, like the very body it clads. Rykiel, like Cixous, fuses the outer with the inner when she claims that the body and the dress are 'mirrored images of each other, each the consecration of the other' (ibid.:103).

Rykiel counters the view that fashion is frivolous, irrational and destructive because it exhibits destabilisation and constant change. Like Roland Barthes, she argues that fashion effects the stopping of time, because the designer compresses past, present and future in every garment, every style (ibid.:107). As Barthes (1985:273) remarks, fashion is a means of keeping vigilance over the present moment: it is a way of erasing history at the very moment of participating in its making. For Rykiel, it seems, fashion functions more like a philosophy or aesthetic which provides both the elements of meaning and the tools for its analysis. This move parallels the denaturalisation of the body and its reconstitution as a look, a feel, an imagined aesthetic.

The ability of fashion to intercede between individuals and the material world in ways that reflect an appropriated aesthetic has long been noted in literature. In Thomas More's *Utopia* (1516), fashion is regarded as a divisive force inimical to equality. More recognises that the 'reckless extravagance' produced by fashion is a practice difficult to restrict. He knew from the failure of sumptuary laws in his own time that a utopian society would have to invent a style of dress that lacked the competitive dynamic of fashion. He therefore prescribed that everyone should wear much the same style, with some variation for sex and marital status (although he does not specify what these would be). All garments would have to be pleasant to look at and give ease of movement.

A modern version of this attitude is expressed in Umberto Eco's essay, 'Lumbar Thoughts' (1986), which argues for the adoption of loose clothing much like a monk's costume in preference to the ubiquitous casual wear of today's jeans and T-shirts. When Eco wore jeans he became increasingly self-conscious of his overweight body. He found jeans too tight in the lumbar region, and this in turn prevented him from engaging in creative, intellectual work. Eco's humorous essay is an opportunity to deride the fashion system as inherently conservative, especially in its support of gender distinctive dress codes, and the anti-intellectualism that is promoted by materialism.

To use dress as a means of creating a social utopia is to emphasise its importance in shaping human consciousness. More and Eco think it is impossible to build a perfect society if people are ill dressed. How that aesthetic choice is made between garments which are regarded as restraining or pleasing, is not, however, considered. In the *New Atlantis*, written by Francis Bacon in 1605, dress is colourful, made of luxurious fabrics such as satin, velvet, linen, silk and feathers, and even encrusted with jewels. It is a form of entertainment, a source of pleasure and amusement. Merged styles which promote cross-dressing and enable women and men to wear a skirt and trousers at the same time are also advocated as aesthetically pleasing forms which freed individuals from restraining conventions (see Ribeiro, 1986).

By the nineteenth century, utopian clothing was less fanciful and exotic, and more related to contemporary styles remodelled by a utilitarian impulse. Utopian dress had evolved into dress reform, where aesthetic considerations still played a part. In *News from Nowhere* (1891), William Morris envisages men in medieval tunics and women in the ancient classical costume; H. G. Wells, in *A Modern Utopia* (1905), dresses both men and women of the ruling class in white tunics with purple bands, although women have in addition a loose, coloured robe. As Ribeiro, a modern historian of costume, wryly remarks, 'it all sounds as though Wells had been looking at contemporary Liberty catalogues' (1992:231). Another instance in which aesthetics are largely overlooked is provided by Aldous Huxley, whose colour-coded garments in the dystopian society of *Brave New World* (1932) replace class insignia, and are worn by both men and women (Ribeiro, 1992:233). In each example, utopian garments are designed to flatter the human form as well as to signify the wearer's social position.

The technique of reading an individual's politics or morality from the way she dresses has circulated through the history of women's social and economic struggles. The wearing of trousers and bloomers, for instance, has been regarded as a blatant signal of female sexual abandon and rebelliousness. Even when women wore these items for practical or health reasons, they were frequently accused of violating their feminine roles and advocating a range of unorthodox, even criminal, practices.

Kate Luck, in her historical review of clothing styles in the American women's movement, gives numerous examples of how the decision to wear bloomers or trousers beneath a full dress was taken as evidence of a wild spirit and radical socialist beliefs (1992:209). Although dress reform had played a prominent part in the feminist movements of the early nineteenth century, it so readily provoked hostile responses from the general public that the struggle for a more practical and healthy form of female clothing became a political liability. Embedded in these events is an unarticulated aesthetic which shapes the look of femininity. Dress styles which violate that aesthetic are interpreted as gestures of renunciation and hostility.

Attempts to abolish tight-laced corsets and to reduce the number and the weight of women's clothes became the basis of a new feminine aesthetic. However, in the mid-nineteenth century, dress reforms such as the adoption of trousers in order to give women freer movement were associated with dangerous political and social upheavals. Luck describes the moral panic created by women's adoption of trousers, and how this contaminated the political reforms and economic ambitions of women's reform movements: 'once "free lovism", which was seen to be an outcome of utopian doctrine, became the focus of a "moral panic", trousered dress became a much less attractive proposition' for women (ibid.:210).

In most cultures, styles of dress and body adornment attempt to produce a different body, that is, to reshape it into an aesthetic and social ideal, whether through scarification, nose and neck-rings, hair dyeing or fashionable garments. The effect of clothing on the constitution of subjectivity, and the use of dress as a cultural metaphor for the body, bring theories of identity formation directly into contact with the regulation of the body. In *Discipline and Punish* (1977), Foucault charts those structural mechanisms which produce a disciplined and passive body, and one of those mechanisms is how the body is clothed. Both the increased use of uniforms in the nineteenth century for military and professional purposes, and the general regulation of clothing for specific occasions such as weddings, funerals and civic ceremonies, suggested to Foucault some of the means by which regimes of discipline were effected in that period.

Elizabeth Wilson adds the contemporary example of women's prison dress. Some penal institutions now permit women to wear their own clothes while incarcerated—not as a reward, but as a means of increasing surveillance. The logic is that when female prisoners wear their own clothes rather than a uniform, they reveal a great deal more of their characters or personalities, thereby giving the authorities useful information about how best to police such women (Wilson, 1992:11). In the late twentieth century, when some dress styles are self-consciously infused with the wearer's aesthetic taste, when garments have become self-referentially fetishised, sexualised and politicised, the point of fashion is to articulate the individual's world-view. As Wilson notes:

> clothing . . . has the unique characteristic of being able to express ideas about sex and the body while simultaneously it actually adorns the body . . . These insights move us away from the simple, moralistic rejection of fashion . . . We can still acknowledge that dress is a powerful weapon of control and dominance, while widening our view to encompass an understanding of its *simultaneously* subversive qualities. (ibid.:12, 14)

Wilson is drawn to the conclusion that fashion need not be about regimentation and restriction. Embracing a style is not always a gesture which undermines the individual while at the same time expanding an already engorged capitalist system. She also argues that the economic exploitation inherent in a consumer-dominated culture will not be reduced simply by putting an end to fashion. Instead, she supports the reverse position, namely that when fashion is understood in aesthetic terms (as a manner of ordering, categorising and enchanting the lived milieu) then simultaneously it assumes a more radical potential. It is a position also advocated by the notorious fashion designer, Vivienne Westwood, who argues that the extension, proliferation and multiplication of styles constitute the more radical act, because it is the plurality of fashions that elevates fashion's value to the individual over that of profits for multinational corporations.

Diane Arbus also acknowledges the importance of fashion as an aesthetic marker, but only in order to argue against what it reveals. Arbus began working in the late 1940s as a fashion photographer with such leading magazines as *Glamour, Harper's Bazaar* and *Vogue.* Her family's business (selling luxury furs and accessories from a Fifth Avenue store in New York City) had immersed her in a world of fashion and consumerism. Wealth, style and decoration were the taken-for-granted components of her ostensibly comfortable world. The style of fashion photography which she developed reinforced that contemporary aesthetic and social perspective. Fashion was about purchasing a lifestyle: it was a transformative device for carrying the fashionable young into the heartland of success and social acceptability. Arbus regarded every fashion-shot as a promise of a happy ending; it contained romantic love, and a protected existence far from the urban dangers of loneliness, crowds and crime (Shloss, 1994:114). It was as if fashionability marked the position from which to claim the rewards of the bourgeois lifestyle. Arbus came to challenge this photographic message that individual needs could be met through material possessions, and that fashion was a means of linking the inner desire for happiness with the external plenitude offered by a middle-class world.

Arbus did not remain long in the fashion world after deciding that its aesthetic was false. Those carefully sculptured images of elite tastes and *haute couture,* which were designed to make both the world and the individual appear beautiful, were better seen as betrayals of aesthetic ideals. Those images, supposedly encapsulating the very best taste, the highest order of cultural capital and the finest instances of human creativity, were on the contrary perverse readings of aesthetic values. Arbus turned instead to those portrait photographs which would make her famous, and produced unfashionable images of damaged and different human beings: sideshow freaks, nudists, twins, transvestites, midgets and giants. These images captured an underworld rarely seen by the mainstream and better suited to her own aesthetic ambitions. Instead of barricading off the ordinary from the threatening faces of the freak, Arbus showed how closely related the ordinary and the freakish are to one another.

Arbus's method was to juxtapose her subjects: wearing the same dress or special hairstyle, one would be a professional model photographed in a fashion studio, and the other photograph (taken in the outside world) would be of a dressed-up 'freak'. The similarities and differences were intended to reveal the degree to which an image could be a disguise. Arbus's photographs demonstrate how the glamorous world of high fashion (where products are sold as elements of a total lifestyle) colludes with the off-beat settings of marginal individuals, who commonly appropriate these same products and infuse them with another, unanticipated character. In both worlds, the body was understood to be simply a device, a tool employed to bring about one's desires. The revelation of Arbus's images can be read as a dual aesthetic: on the one hand, an appreciation of stylised beauty in appearance, and on the other a fascination with its falsity and inauthenticity. Arbus demonstrates that the surface, that which is readily seen, must be understood simultaneously as artifice.

Her portrait photographs of people, whether ordinary or extraordinary, are deliberately framed so as to disrupt and reverse the status quo, thereby making every image appear both strange and conventional. Fashionable objects like dresses, long gloves, and winged eye-glasses remain the same whether they are located in a *Vogue* magazine or a transvestite's backstage dressing-room. Their resilience confirms Arbus's view that fashion is a duplicitous mechanism which creates a false world. This is vividly illustrated in photographs of the same fashion object placed awkwardly in the unglamorous context of an outcast person's habitat. Even here the object promises, however inappropriately, that happiness and success can be purchased with the bourgeois lifestyle. In this manner, fashion is demonstrably about artifice: it does not matter whether the fashionable tableau is constructed in the contrived setting of a photographer's studio or in the private realms of fashion *habitués* who wish to transform themselves and to materialise their fantasies by possessing fashionable objects. Fashion is artifice, and we are forced to confront this unavoidable viewpoint when individuals' dress and accessory selections are revealed through the unrelenting photographic lens to be unflattering and unsuitable for them.

Arbus's confronting photographs represent the psychic isolation and deadening atmosphere created by bourgeois life. In these images she has recast the normal into the perfidious, and the unusual into the real. Clothing functions less as a protection and form of enhancement for those wearing it than as a disciplinary device which controls or even oppresses the wearer. Fashionable clothes do not fulfil their promise to transport those who wear them into the acceptable and cushioned bourgeois world; instead, they betray and falsify the ideal of the real self. Shloss (1994:123) gives as an example Arbus's photograph of triplets dressed identically. When their conventional and almost prim outfits are worn by a single person, the look is innocent, appropriate and easy. But when identical triplets wear the same clothes, their bodies speak louder than their dress. Their uncanny existence makes fashion seem a failure; although it tries to marshal them into conventionality, their trebled body remains unresponsive. Simply to wear a fashionable outfit will not guarantee the idealised lifestyle that it advertises: it will certainly not demystify this particularly freakish phenomenon. At such moments, the body is recognised as resistant to those reshapings which fashionability attempts to induce. The uniformed triplets speak of an unimagined realm beyond the fashionable, which remains impervious to cultural interventions. Fashion suggests that we all share an aesthetic constructed of culturally meaningful artefacts but every now and again bodies refuse to be remade in the image of an aesthetic ideal. The genetically variable body is an obdurate reality which neither fashion models nor fashion *habitués* can overlook. For Arbus, then, fashion is an overlay, a form of armour designed to cover the recalcitrant body.

Baudrillard (1993) views fashion as economic in origin and aesthetic in its effects. Like Arbus, he sees a continuity between the urge to consume and the disappointment of possession. This is particularly apparent in New Age fashions, where environmentalism and other liberal causes become ambiguously implicated in the capitalist enterprise. As Lipovetsky points out, the seductiveness of fashion 'coexists with the arms race, with lack of personal security in daily life, with the economic crisis and the subjective crisis' (1994:132). Baudrillard understands the desire to extract aesthetic satisfactions from everyday life since, without such pleasures, it can be a grinding monotony. However, fashion's promise of relief from this, as Arbus shows, is unreliable. In a distinctive move away from conventional explanations of fashion as a symbolic reinstatement of class divisions, Baudrillard describes how we are all encouraged to become consumers as a just measure of social merit, although, for some, consumption is a compensation for the failure of the social and political system to provide opportunities for individual liberation and satisfaction. Consumption can be marketed as a means of buying happiness when one's own aesthetic satisfaction is not presumed to be the same as everyone else's. The latent promise of the consumer revolution is that by extending the distribution of a wide range of goods, a degree of personal pleasure will be experienced by everybody.

The Benetton fashion company fully understands the new consumer mood in which individuals seek personal pleasure, psychological gratification and aesthetic rewards from their purchases. Benetton has introduced the idea that fashion spending can be part of a new political platform which is sympathetic to the ambitions of various eco-movements, as well as to anti-racism, anti-sexism and those forms of local politics which advocate national pride and tribalism. Benetton associates political correctness with consumer commodities by successfully blurring the boundaries between images of real social events and representations of a restructured and utopian world where Benetton's 'united colors' suggest a strengthened globalism (Giroux, 1993–94). It is when fashionability is dislodged from its material foundations and recast as an aesthetic formation that it can become a source of self-administered individual satisfaction.

Elizabeth Wilson (1992) regards fashion as a device which pulls together the fragmented aspects of modern identity, and provides the individual with a means of negotiating the often incoherent aspects of the everyday. Fashion can function ideologically by formally resolving, at the imaginary level, the social contradictions produced by modern, urban living. At the same time it can express the moral location of an individual by signifying repudiation or reconciliation. Individuals can dress in order to criticise the dominant culture and to transcend its homogenising influences while at the same time aligning themselves with other marginalised and equally critical groups. In these ways, fashion provides a sense of location even for those individuals whose social critique distances them from the mainstream.

Fashion can relocate the experience of pleasure outside the restrictions of a private realm. Pleasure can be embodied in the parading, advertising and public flaunting of the very quest for pleasure. With practices such as these, fashion becomes a means of self-adornment and self-attention, as well as a means of influencing the opinions of others. It allows individuals to embody their aesthetic positions in the styles of their choice—as cool, rich, bohemian, feminine, queer or whatever. To map the different fashions is to enumerate the various aesthetic pleasures attached to being fashionable.

7

Fashion Sense

> *[Clothes] change our view of the world and the world's view of us . . . there is much to support the view that it is clothes that wear us and not we them.*
>
> Virginia Woolf

When Una Troubridge sat for her portrait by the painter Romaine Brooks, she selected masculine dress. In her everyday life she was more likely to wear conventional feminine dress, in contrast to the more masculine attire of her partner, Radclyffe Hall. In the portrait, however, she would be figured alone, without her partner, and so to communicate her sexuality she dressed in masculine clothes. Violet Trefusis and Vita Sackville-West did much the same when they escaped together for a short-lived honeymoon in Paris. Violet wore feminine dress and Vita masculine clothes in order to live out their relationship in the public domain. This gender masquerade allowed the couple to experience in public some of the privileges of the heterosexual, as well as signalling to those in the know who they really were. On their return home to England, both reverted to conventional feminine dress (Rolley, 1992:37; Leaska and Phillips, 1989:115).

In the early decades of the twentieth century, when the existence of lesbians was rigorously effaced, clothing could be used as a way of identifying its wearers, and in many instances, such dress codes worked to bind individuals into a self-conscious subculture. Katrina Rolley (1990) points out that early twentieth-century lesbians dressed in styles that both signified their sexual orientation and suppressed any knowledge of it. By adopting similar modes of dress, women could appear to be sisters and therefore part of a conventional familial grouping, concealing their sexual relationship from unsuspecting onlookers. Alternatively, by wearing stylised masculine and feminine garments, they could demonstrate the opposite, and enable others in the know to acknowledge what was before their eyes.

The use of clothing to designate gender appropriateness and to exploit the opportunities this creates for masquerade underlies an important element in the deployment of fashion, namely, that clothing speaks to both strangers and observers. Styles in appearance simultaneously attract and deflect attention. When clothes are misappropriated, as in gender-bending, they fracture conventions; when they are parodied, they satirise those same conventions for allocating clothing in accordance with strict divisions between the feminine and masculine. Particular kinds of clothes allow the wearer to pass as a member of the other sex in the eyes of uninitiated observers; to knowledgeable spectators, the cross-dressed communicate pleasure and play. An example of the pleasures of coded dress styles is Vivienne Westwood's 'Half-dressed City Gent' outfit, an ensemble which has women wearing men's shirts (but with dishevelled collar and necktie askew) and tight pantihose with either a fig leaf appliqued to the crotch or a 'graffiti'd' penis:

> I wear my Vivienne Westwood (half-dressed city gent) knickers, with a penis graffiti'd on the front. No one knows. I am aware, going into a Board meeting, of a hidden gender transformation, and am all the more confident of its significance in the ignorance of others. As the transvestite acknowledges to himself the feel of the silk cami-knickers under the grey suit, so I, female, relish my secret metamorphosis—the potential for audaciousness—in a world of drab conventions. (Ash, 1992:184)

It is popular to view modern, urban society as an economy of symbolic goods, which individuals attempt to manipulate in order to establish themselves. Fashion is part of this struggle, in so far as it offers opportunities to name and claim what is considered valuable. Bourdieu (1984) calls those who can succeed in doing so the taste-makers, or cultural intermediaries. These individuals engage in competition in order to monopolise goods. In turn, this positions them to open new channels of communication and to circulate information between formerly separated social categories. Those in the fashion, retailing and advertising industries function as cultural intermediaries by carrying niche knowledge from one social realm to another.

In one sense, fashion is an organisation of knowledge based on restricted access to goods and services. Levels of fashionability depend upon differential access to knowledge of what is 'hot' and what is not. An ever-changing supply of commodities may give the illusion that such knowledge is unrestricted. But more often than not, possession of it is governed by the individual's awareness of other knowledges, say, about what constitutes 'legitimate' taste and its hierarchies, and what is appropriate. How individuals acquire such information is contingent on a variety of circumstances.

In the popular British television comedy 'Absolutely Fabulous', which stars Joanna Lumley and Jennifer Saunders, a recurring motif in a sketch about the end-of-year fashion sales is the value of labelled clothes. The character Edina Monsoon constantly repeats the instruction, 'Names, darling, names'. Consuming *per se* has no social value. To buy an object discounted up to 90 per cent may seem enticing, but in fact yields dismal rewards, because a no-name cheap item has no social currency. The Ab Fab buyers know that value resides only in the name of the product. This exemplifies the importance of niche knowledge. Wealth alone, the ability to purchase, is not sufficient to make one fashionable. Lacroix has a certain currency that the identical (but no-name) imitation totally lacks. Astute consumers must know what to search for, what to desire, and how to identify goods that will position them *à la mode*. Their chances of recognising the fashionable when they encounter it will reflect the extent of their cultural capital, that is, their knowledge of taste (Bourdieu, 1984).

Ironically, however, fashion can make the acquisition of cultural capital even more difficult. It can identify the amount that one needs in order to read and to appreciate the new and esoteric, but frequently only after the fashionable moment has passed. For instance, given the right knowledge and group affiliations, one can see that what appears to be a pile of rocks in a prestigious museum is in actuality a modern sculpture. But by the time this knowledge has filtered out to various social groups, the aesthetic which produced it has changed. Fashion appears to make available the means of acquiring cultural capital in the form of illustrated magazines, self-improvement courses and reading guides which promise to place consumers at the 'cutting edge'. However, since these items are themselves designed for mass consumption, they may not help one to acquire cultural capital. The residual problem for consumers is that the marketing and commodification of the desirable—especially when it happens to be fashionability itself— is directed primarily toward profitability. To read *Face* will not ensure the individual's fashionability, but to be unaware of the magazine would in certain circles diminish the claim to fashionable status.

Baudrillard (1993) depicts modern society as an inherently disordered cultural universe, where a flood of signs and images produces pastiche and irony, as well as saturating the individual in conditions which often make stable meanings impossible. The different styles and labels of fashionable goods (which are used as classificatory symbols) and the various symbolic systems which give a sense of order and stability are also the very same features that maintain the arbitrariness of the social world. Whether it is high or low, establishment or marginal, fashion is part of the 'dream world', according to Baudrillard: it is a dimension of reality constructed from images, and as such it restates the aleatoric, random character of contemporary society. These dream worlds (the name itself is often attached to department stores, theme parks and even Hollywood) elevate the personal enjoyment of immediate, sensory and bodily pleasures over those identified by philosophers such as Plato and Immanuel Kant as 'pure' and 'universal'. The seductiveness of such dream worlds allegedly opposes that rational mode of appreciation which attempts to disengage and distance itself from sensually seductive experiences. In other words, the very methods which encourage critique and the accumulation of cultural capital can be obscured by the attractions of the immediate and sensory. Fashion is in this respect a form of anti-intellectual seduction.

But fashion is not concerned unequivocally with conformity and sensuousness. Some social groups repudiate mainstream fashion by developing oppositional systems of knowledge. 'Anti-fashion' refers usually to a style of dress which falls outside the organised system of fashion change, but which, none the less, is self-conscious. Indifference to fashion is found among the least socially powerful, namely the young, the aged, the institutionalised and those who have little or no control over their appearances. Anti-fashion is distinguishable from indifference to fashion because it always remains in dialogue with the fashionable. Ironically, the fashion industry often appropriates the styles of the anti-fashionists. Street-style, for example, has been incorporated into designer fashions for the mass markets. But although such counter-fashions are vulnerable to appropriation, they serve a purpose, particularly for marginal or subcultural groups. They enable the development of a coherent look which uses current fashion in order to articulate social opposition and alternative identities.

Rosalind Coward argues that fashion cannot be read adequately unless one moves beyond the popular view that fashion is merely about annual changes in colours, styles, shapes and accessories. Fashion is much more revealing as a key to analysing the present moment: 'one thing that fashion is quite categorically *not* is an expression of individuality', Coward writes, because fashion 'is always the acceptance of the prevailing ideals' (1984:29). Claims that street-style or grunge or New Age indicate actual breaks with the status quo are treated sceptically by Coward, who regards such phenomena as merely new categories of fashion. She maintains that there are hierarchies of fashion but no repudiations of it. The premier position is occupied by styles that connote 'wealth through the ideas of elegance and sophistication of tastes' (ibid.:30). Emphasis is given here to the intrinsic qualities of garments, especially the textiles used and how they have been tailored. This makes silk, suede and fine cotton the most valuable textiles for garments because they can be worn directly against the skin. These elements engender the 'classic' fashion style, which is supposed to survive changes of seasons and resist the novel and popular appeal of merely 'classy' garments whose trend-setter images suggest that they are a class ahead of the rest. The knowledgeable fashion *habitué* understands that fashion occupies the centre by advocating what the predominant culture holds most valuable.

Fashion is about the ordering and categorising of the individual's knowledge of certain cultural formations. Certain fashions do not fully obscure real social and cultural divisions despite their popularity. When an obviously working-class appropriation of upper-class fashions takes place, it is commonly assumed that a homogenising of interests has also occurred. The popular imitation of styles is seen as a dilution, as if the novel claims of the originals were inevitably toned down in cheaper versions. As the cheaper versions of *haute couture*, popular fashions are supposedly favoured by those unwilling to be too innovative and distinguished. These ideas about the trickle-down of upper-class styles into lower-class mass markets derive from the theories of Veblen and Simmel (discussed in Chapter 2), and assume that the majority of people have a shared interest in middle-class tastes. Such perspectives prevent us seeing fashion as a segmented phenomenon that is part of various local knowledge systems.

Partington (1992) argues that fashion can rearticulate class differences and express class conflicts, even when it appears that the dominant tastes of the upper classes have been transmitted directly to those below. She contends that subordinate groups preserve class divisions by developing their own aesthetics instead of merely absorbing those of the upper echelons. She uses masculine and feminine styles to exemplify the relationship between class domination and consumerism. Working-class men who wear the common uniform of the business suit are more readily seen as subversive because they appropriate it only for specific occasions such as weddings and funerals. Although the suit may disguise their class position momentarily, it does not dilute their working-class interests. Women from the same class, however, are less resistant. They appear to capitulate to the middle class because their consumption of fashion imitates dominant tastes.

During the relatively affluent decades of the 1950s and 1960s, every social stratum was seen as a potential consumer market. Women in particular were being pursued as good consumers, and their 'desiring gaze' was cultivated by retailers. Women were more vulnerable than men to the new marketing techniques, which taught them that the acquisition of taste was a means of social betterment. The idea is appropriated from Veblen's (1899) depiction of the wives of successful men, who consumed conspicuously in order to demonstrate their husband's financial achievements. Women's appearances were the signs of newly acquired wealth. However, as a target of new consumer practices in the mid-twentieth century, the acquisitiveness of women did not necessarily indicate any actual changes in social location. It may well be the case that because women shop more, they are the more active consumers, but this does not signify that class differences are thereby being eroded.

Partington argues that mass markets and patterns of gendered consumption are better seen as techniques employed by the fashion and leisure industries in the pursuit of profit: 'the development of a mass-market fashion system enabled class-specific groups to be targeted as consumers, and relied increasingly on gender-specific consumer skills' (1992:149). The existence of a mass market does not necessarily entail a diffusion of dominate tastes and values, but rather the invention of new styles of class identification which exist simultaneously in various social strata. Consequently, that diffusion of tastes which accounts for the prevalence of similar styles over a broad spectrum is better explained as a 'trickle-across' than a 'trickle-down' effect. Whatever distinctions can be made between fashion garments and practices, they subtly identify various self-defined groups.

More influential than class identification in attracting purchasers is the role of fashion professionals such as commentators, magazine editors or retail buyers, who are in a position, as Bourdieu (1984) observes, to shape the tastes and consuming habits of specific audiences. These entrepreneurial figures have emerged since the 1950s, and played a crucial part in restructuring the market-place. Now there is little imitation of one group by another, in a Veblenesque manner; more often, the impetus for changes comes from within each group as fashion innovators constantly experiment with new styles. As Partington describes, 'class differences do not disappear in this system, on the contrary more complex and multiple differences are made possible through increasingly elaborate and complex manufacturing, media and retailing strategies' (ibid.:151).

Numerous examples show that fashion fails to produce a homogeneous aesthetic. Particular groups have their enduring fashion styles which parallel mainstream conventions, such as the afro hairstyle for African Americans, the colour codes for Hispanic Americans, and western clothes for gay men. Each illustrates how a subcultural identification, resting on local knowledges, undercuts many prevailing fashion styles. There are other instances of appearances being used as a means of counter-cultural assault. The long hair, beads and floral styles of the hippies; the shaved hair and black-leather garb of skinheads; the torn jeans and chain accessories of bikies—all these examples of unconventional dress aim in part at affronting the bourgeoisie. It is the irony of fashion that each of these styles—the romantic pastoralism of the hippies, say, or the S/M nihilism of the punks—has slowly been appropriated by the fashion industries and sold back to the middle classes.

This is not to assert that fashion must always fail as a form of resistance. Even if it serves for only a limited period of time as a vehicle for individual and group expression, fashion can succeed in supplying a language or framework from which parodic and subversive ideas can take shape (Hebdige, 1979, 1988; Appadurai, 1990). The multinational corporations whose interests suppress diversities and local knowledges can be deflected from their purposes by the appropriation of their products. When jeans, Coca-Cola, McDonald's or Mickey Mouse are symbolically recycled in order to build local and diverse cultural knowledges, then the hegemony of fashion is further undermined (Davis, 1992:199).

The success of fashion in contributing to the production of local or niche knowledge adds credibility to the early theories of Georg Simmel, as discussed in Chapter 2, who posited that fashion is a technique for distinguishing oneself in an urban environment where the old rules pertaining to class divisions no longer make sense. In the new and unregulated metropolis, people are free to invent themselves and to aspire or to pretend to be what they are not. As a theory of urban consumerism, Simmel's is a better account than the one offered by his classical counterpart Thorstein Veblen (1899), who regards fashion, as described previously, as a technique for ·preserving class divisions and consolidating their internal cohesion. Veblen's argument that the upper class was forced to invent fashion in order to maintain superiority rests upon an assumed immobility of social structure. He understood that everyone wants to be in the upper class. Simmel, in contrast, imagined society as more fluid, and that fashion emerges from the coherency of segmented groups with highly specific knowledge systems. With hindsight, Simmel seems the more sophisticated analyst in understanding that access to every kind of fashion would not necessarily result in a single style becoming dominant. As is now obvious, the greater availability of goods has led to a proliferation of markets, each with its own niche knowledge or fashion sense about styles and appearances. These systems of identification have encouraged the refinement of distinctions between products. They have essentially customised all fashionable items and created differences in what appear otherwise to be very similar objects.

8

Consuming Fashion

[So many know] the price of everything, and the value of nothing.

Oscar Wilde

When the US press arrived in Paris in 1944, after the city had been liberated from its occupation by the Nazis, they were surprised to discover the *haute couture* industry alive and well. The fact that the German occupation of Paris in World War II from 1940 until 1944 had not damaged the fashion industries created international outrage. Until the late 1940s those who had been employed in the industry continued to be accused of collaboration with the enemy, and such indictments threatened to destroy the French hegemony over fashion (Taylor, 1992:135). Despite hardships created by the war (such as the loss of experienced and skilled staff, the shortage of fabrics and the serious rationing of utilities) the production of luxury fabrics and goods had continued. When the Nazi army first occupied Paris in 1940 it was expected that the fashion houses would be closed. This did not happen because the Nazis took over the culture and economy of Paris with the intention of making them contribute to the Third Reich. The highly developed French fashion industry had its profits siphoned into the treasury of the German government, helping to finance the Nazi invasion of France and the continuation of war in Europe.

'What place was there for luxury clothing in a conquered, demoralised, occupied and chaotic country?' asks Lou Taylor (1992:128–9). Although a few of the elite fashion houses were closed, the vast majority stayed open for business throughout the Occupation. This was remarkable, given the drastically changed conditions for conducting business. The clientele, for instance, was no longer international but restricted to local beneficiaries of the invading regime. Jean Patou, Jeanne Lanvin, Nina Ricci, Charles Worth and others were able to keep their salons open throughout the Occupation because they accepted these new clients and joined the social life of the collaborationists. Coco Chanel closed her business but remained prominently in support of the Third Reich for much of the war (ibid.:131).

This history of Parisian *haute couture* is significant for showing how important fashion had become as an economic enterprise, and how serious a contribution it made to France's economy. But it indicates in addition how alluring fashion is to the consumer, and how political and social exigencies can be offset by the pleasures it promises. Given that fashion is not driven solely by economics, it is worth asking what consumers imagine they are acquiring when they purchase fashionable items.

By the late 1930s the Parisian fashion world was contributing so hugely to the French economy that the two systems were virtually intertwined. Fashion had become dominant largely through the democratisation of its products. The Parisian fashion houses were no longer concerned only with *haute couture* and handmade garments. They had successfully incorporated into their businesses cosmetics, perfumes, fashion accessories and ready-to-wear clothes, thereby making themselves available to the middle classes and, in turn, pivotal to the French economy. Had these industries closed down during World War II, the French economy would never have recovered: hence the justification for collaborating with the fascist regime (Taylor, 1992).

Now that the economics of fashion are global, the dominance of Paris as fashion's epicentre has weakened, and the centralised and aristocratic character of nineteenth-century *haute couture* has been transformed. While some of its structures have survived into the late twentieth century, such as the professional creator or designer, seasonal collections, and live fashion parades with models in sumptuous outfits, a further level of organisational development has been added. In the 1920s, at the height of *haute couture*, the house of Jean Patou employed 1300 people in its workshops; Chanel was bigger with 2500 employees, and Dior employed 1200 until the 1950s. But by 1985 the combined employment figure for twenty-one elite fashion houses was only 2000, and their clients included only 3000 women world-wide (Lipovetsky, 1994:88–9).

The economic survival of the elite fashion houses has been assured by their diversification from handmade garments. Although Chanel, Patou and Lanvin sold perfumes in the 1920s, this did not become the staple of the fashion industries until the late 1970s. From this moment, perfumes, cosmetics, fashion accessories and the licensing of the fashion label to be applied to other items (such as leather goods, tableware, pens, underwear and cigarette lighters) became the source of profitability. *Haute couture* creations still attract the attention of the world press, but the financial success of these fashion houses rests elsewhere.

By the mid 1980s Yves Saint Laurent was deriving much of its profits from the royalties brought in from licensing. In the next decade, fashion houses like Pierre Cardin, Nina Ricci and Dior earned more from their royalties than from direct production (ibid.:89). In addition to marketing fashion accessories, they developed ready-to-wear clothes, which bore the prestigious label but, unlike the originals, were not made to order. In 1994 Lacoste produced more than twenty-three million items of clothing which were sold in eighty countries. The company's annual turnover in 1994 was \$US700 million (*Age*, 1994:16). From 1982 to 1986 NEXT retail stores in England increased their pre-tax profits from £4 million to £92 million. During the 1980s the design business (which included fashion clothing) trebled its activities, expanding at a rate of almost 25 per cent per annum (Shields, 1992:168n20).

Fashion has been called a western phenomenon, intricately tied to developments in consumerism and industrialisation. Consumerism is invoked to explain a great many social changes which transformed the west from the sixteenth century to the present. Theorists such as Emile Durkheim, Max Weber, Karl Marx and Ferdinand Tönnies trace back, to an era of social eruption and transformation, socio-historical events such as class restructuring, labour patterns, religious reformation, upon which modern democracy came to be founded. The consumer revolution has been recognised as an important restructuring force which differs dramatically from more commonly acknowledged sources of social change such as war and religious zealotry. Material abundance has transformed societies, and continues to do so as a ubiquitous form of social change. The consumer revolution is still both a destabilising and reconstituting force in every market economy. It has intensified social disorganisation by disrupting the visible social hierarchies of the pre-industrial feudal order, but it has also reconstituted a more homogeneous society by democratising luxuries and raising the standards of living of the majority (McCracken, 1988).

Exactly when consumerism began is a matter of some dispute. The French historian associated with the *Annales* school, Fernand Braudel (1973), dates it back to the fifteenth century, Chandra Mukerji (1983) to the sixteenth, Neil McKendrick (1982) to the eighteenth, and Rosalind Williams (1982) to the nineteenth. The term 'consumerism' commonly denotes the pursuit of manufactured goods, which is why the growth of consumerism is often linked with the development of industrialism. Other forms of consumerism, however, signify the desire to possess goods of an esoteric and unique character. Mukerji (1983) and Braudel (1973) both argue that consumerism pre-dates capitalism, in so far as there have always been goods whose values and meanings are symbolic rather than economic. For example, some goods are valued because of their capacity to develop a patina over time. Family portraiture is an example: such paintings are valued as proof of an individual's noble lineage (McCracken, 1988:12–13). Here the satisfaction of consumer interests takes on a different dimension, since it involves acknowledging that some objects have idiosyncratic cultural significances over and above their material value.

Braudel (1973) notes that new practices of consumerism were visible in the court cultures of both Renaissance Italy and late sixteenth-century Elizabethan England. In both instances, extravagant displays of wealth at court involved conspicuous wastage of valued resources such as food, clothing and luxury goods. These were used to demonstrate the superiority of the monarch and his or her extraordinary (that is, religious and transcendent) power. Such ostentation was also used to cultivate a sense of dependency upon the monarch as the fount from which status, wealth and power were dispensed. Mukerji (1983) argues that Elizabeth I's display of extravagance was a political strategy which forced the nobility at court to participate in a system of power exchanges that undermined their own interests. The aristocratic class was kept in debt so its members could not afford to organise a challenge to the monarch. This dynamic still operates with fashion today. The expense of pursuing the fashionable can be so great as to prevent other forms of acquisition, such as the development of cultural capital, that could produce a significant improvement in the individual's social circumstances.

Different styles in consumerism and the development of competing fashions became more visible with the social changes emanating from various court societies. The most obvious change was in the differentiation of tastes. Formerly, it may have been safely assumed, as Veblen has argued and as discussed in the previous chapter, that those lower on the social scale would desire the possessions and styles of those above them. However, as more goods became available, and exchanges between societies increased, differences in styles, tastes, aesthetic preferences and attitudes proliferated. It was no longer a matter of the haves being envied by the have-nots. Particularly with the development of a middle class, the consumer preferences of the aristocracy were more likely to be regarded with suspicion than envy, and expressions of hostility and prejudice drew attention to the gaps widening between social classes.

Veblen's account of fashions drifting down from higher to lower classes was propelled by the subordinate's desire for imitation and the superordinate's desire for differentiation. In some instances, however, the tastes of one class were viewed by outsiders as foreign affectations, and the expression of unnatural and decadent proclivities. The divisions of taste, which corresponded roughly to a high-class and low-class structure, had the effect of sequestering social groups from one another. Observable differences in patterns of consumption could then be seen as reflecting the growing distances between the social strata. The envy and awe with which the subordinate had traditionally viewed the superordinate was subsequently overlaid with contempt, disdain and confusion. According to McCracken, this state of affairs was not ameliorated before the eighteenth century, when industrialism made goods more readily available (1988:15–18).

In these early forms of consumerism, we can detect some characteristics of the fashion impulse which have persisted into the contemporary era. In early instances of conspicuous consumption, the attraction of goods purchased or commissioned did not necessarily improve the material conditions of either family or household. Consumption had more to do with symbolic than actual value; many of the desired goods lacked the capacity to acquire 'patina', that is, they would not increase in value with the passage of time or the ministrations of tradition. They were goods designed for display as devices which somehow enhanced their owner. Before industrialism, the skills required to manufacture goods added to their value; over time, they would acquire even more value. But with the development of mass manufacture in the industrial age, the patinated value of goods was immediately lost.

McKendrick nominates the eighteenth century as the origin of the consumer era because it was only with the expansion and availability of manufactured goods that the consumer explosion could take place. For McKendrick, fashion begins with a consumer revolution based on status competition. He links fashionable consumption directly with class changes. The new bourgeoisie expressed a strong demand for new goods which, in turn, promoted the democratisation of fashion. New marketing techniques came into existence, and these generated a speedier diffusion of fashionable ideas. Furthermore, the greater availability of cheaper materials (such as cottons and muslins from India) combined with new entrepreneurial practices (such as those of Josiah Wedgwood, who manipulated tastes in order to create market demands) contributed to an intensified interest in consumption.

The greater variety and number of goods available was matched by a greater number of people actively purchasing them. This created an atmosphere of competing tastes and self-conscious ownership, which McKendrick describes as follows:

> what men and women had once hoped to inherit from their parents, they now expected to buy for themselves. What were once bought at the dictate of need, were now bought at the dictate of fashion. What were once bought for life, might now be bought several times over . . . As a result 'luxuries' came to be seen as mere 'decencies', and 'decencies' came to be seen as 'necessities'. (1982:1)

Concurrent with this revolution in consumer behaviour was a revolution in sensibilities. The increasing rates of consumption represented 'a triumph of style over utility, of aesthetics over function' (McCracken, 1988:19). Where once the value of goods was deemed inherent, it was now contextual. Patina was replaced by novelty as the measure of value. From the eighteenth century onwards, when markets for goods were expanding greatly and the individual enjoyed a far wider choice, divisions between upper-class and lower-class taste became in many instances less obvious. The greater prosperity and growth of the middle classes tended to reduce these aesthetic and economic gaps. Consumer practices functioned as symbolic expressions of social identity, and created social interests between individuals who were otherwise strangers to one another. In this respect, consumerism acquired sociological significance. In cities populated by anonymous strangers, a modern society coalesces largely because certain shared cultural values concerning goods provide for a more cohesive and self-maintaining sociality. Consumerism became a way of life and the basis of societal organisation.

The consumer revolution has changed society and the conduct of its members, but how it does so is difficult to specify. How do objects become the repositories of human desire, and how do they become imbued with cultural meaning? How is social status elevated or deflated by possessions, and how does it enter into competitive relationships with other and similar objects? These aspects of the fashion dynamic have produced various explanations. For instance, we cannot understand the qualities which seem to inhere in a specific object and make it desirable simply by ascribing status to them, for to do so would be to privilege the cost of the item over its cultural or aesthetic value. Such utilitarian approaches have been countered by various psychological, historical and sociological alternatives. For example, Émile Zola (1883), Michael Miller (1981) and Rosalind Williams (1982) have identified the nineteenth-century department store as a site of instruction for the bourgeoisie, whose desires for goods were permeated with new interests in taste and aesthetic knowledge. These stores not only provided incentives for conspicuous consumption, they resulted in a new social hierarchy based on aesthetics rather than property. Fashionability tempered the enthusiasm of those new middle classes who were voracious purchasers of goods but lacked the aesthetic standards by which to judge their value. Consumption without judgement was regarded as banal by such emerging elites of taste as the Regency dandies, who appropriated fashion as a means of distinguishing themselves.

The nineteenth-century dandy dressed with excessive care, and in marked contrast to the extravagance of the aristocracy and the imitative enthusiasm of the bourgeoisie. The dandy was an early devotee of the idea that clothes make the person (Moers, 1960), although not in the customary ways: the function of dandified clothing was not to reflect but to challenge the traditional social hierarchy. The dandy used appearances to invent a new social order by investing goods, clothing, and personal demeanour with cultural significance. The look, the pastimes and the street-style of the individual constituted a new discourse for articulating recent modes of consumption. This marked the beginning of experimentation in what McCracken describes as 'the exploitation of the expressive, cultural power of goods' (1988:27).

The nineteenth century was the period in which the significance of fashion came to be more widely understood in both economic and cultural terms. Not only were new marketing and production techniques being developed, but new theoretical accounts were also being debated in order to explain an increasingly apparent social revolution. For Simmel (1971a), fashion is impelled by the human characteristic to imitate, which was amplified by the class structure and the opportunities for social mobility made available by a metropolitan environment. Most susceptible to the lure of fashion are individuals in the 'insecure classes', especially women, who lack the means of acquiring economic independence. Such individuals want to imitate the fashions and styles of those they perceive to be their betters in order to escape their own insecure situation. In turn, imitative hounds snapping at the heels of the well-turned-out compel fashion leaders to be innovative in asserting their differences from those crowding in upon them.

In analysing the modern mercantile society, Simmel (1978) argues that the culture of money frees individuals from personal dependence on others simply by democratising social distinctions. At the same time, it intensifies the instrumental transactions between individuals by mediating social exchanges through the display of goods, and it justifies the pursuit of certain practices and possessions in terms of their tangible money-value. In such a culture, people develop a blasé attitude toward one another. The pursuit of fashion furthers this tendency. Fashion sufficiently differentiates individuals from one another to intensify competition and mutual awareness but, ironically, encourages desires to resemble one another and to conform to shared pleasures.

The dynamics of fashion in Simmel's account mediate between a series of ambivalences or contrary human tendencies: these include the need for both 'individualisation' and 'equalisation', a sense of union and of segregation, and a desire for dependence on the one hand and freedom on the other. Because fashion allows the individual to balance these contradictory impulses, it also provides a means for enriching our everyday lives. Simmel acknowledges the social value of fashion as an impetus for social improvement; as fashion incorporates social change, and as social change is more often than not an improvement, then fashion is desirable.

By contrast, Thorstein Veblen (1899) sees fashion as a mechanism for maintaining the status quo. In an era of mass production, standardisation comes to reign, and the individuation of both goods and people correspondingly declines. As a result, pseudo-individuality emerges, which is a product of conspicuous consumption. The pursuit of individuality through fashion purchases must be equally unsuccessful both for the wealthy (who consume ostentatiously and wastefully) and for the middle classes, who with less discretionary income consume objects to imitate their social superiors. To Veblen, consumption and the lust for acquisition are wasteful and irrational gestures, which signify the very antithesis of civilisation. He favours instead the puritan work ethic which concentrates on production and accumulation, and in this way he gives no real account of the pleasures that are repeatedly found in routine consumption.

In a modern democracy, the mass production of goods provides the circumstances in which to pursue mass-marketed pleasures. Fashion here becomes a specific kind of pleasure, commonly associated with asserting identity, differentiating oneself from others and exhibiting a sense of superiority. Somewhat perversely, as the barriers between the upper and lower levels of society break down and the once unbridgeable gap between the aristocracy and the bourgeoisie is closed, then a proliferation of artefacts, practices and signs attempts to recreate differences in status and identity.

It then becomes obvious that the democratisation of consumerism produces neither greater social harmony nor an elevation of cultural and aesthetic interests. Instead, the upward striving and downward self-distancing movements produced by fashion maintain a self-generating dynamic. As signs of luxury become more readily available, a consumer-oriented economy must continue to manufacture more and more objects of desire in order to sustain itself. This is an economic fundamental. When applied to social relations, however, this energetic circulation of goods—legitimated as fashion—translates into a form of sociability based on the individual's 'readings' of one another from the superficial signs of displayed goods. One consequence of this kind of sociability is to create opportunities for, first, the self-fashioning and then the manipulation of one's image and social role.

Fashion creates a world filled with goods heavily laden with symbolic value and culturally idiosyncratic meanings. Fashion requires shoppers to be semioticians skilled at reading the subtle signs and commentaries encoded in fashionable objects. A function of department stores is to provide some of this necessary instruction. Indeed, the nineteenth-century department store was a repository of instruction; it assumed the position of social primer and self-consciously provided individuals with the kind of knowledge required to discern the fashionability, attractiveness and value of various new products.

The arrival of the department store contributed importantly to the growth of the fashion industries. Women of all classes could venture into the public domain as shoppers, if not for the first time then certainly in greater numbers. The freedom to enter department stores and commercial centres in order to view the displays of purchasable goods provided women shoppers with social opportunities similar to those enjoyed by men in other public contexts. The woman as consumer became anonymous yet mobile; she could legitimately leave the house in order to seek out her desires and encounter at will the unknown and unexpected. As consumers, Victorian women could escape their confining domestic spheres, experience a sense of self-direction in the pursuit of pleasure and discover a source of self-definition remote from the sequestered world in which they were immersed back home.

The nineteenth-century department store is also a useful index to how men and women diverged from one another as consumers. While the department store welcomed women and gave them social opportunities they previously lacked, it was also there that the 'pathologising' of the public woman became most apparent. As noted in Chapter 5, Zola's novel *Ladies' Delight* describes how definitions of the feminine came to be linked with such psychological disturbances as the new department-store madness, kleptomania. As the modern world became more affluent and prone to overproduction, excess and indulgence, the practices of everyday life, such as shopping, were identified as sources of instability, even of insanity. The belief that modern life was riven by desires and excessive intensities, generated by increasing opportunities for experimentation and temptation, created a pathogenic environment in which the weak were seen as becoming weaker. Women were regarded as particularly vulnerable. As consumers who were constantly in contact with the articles of temptation, women became associated with modern urban pathology. Their desire to consume was believed to link the motifs of the ungovernable and unruly with that of the feminine.

Rachel Bowlby (1985) describes the persistence of this bifurcated characterisation of male and female shoppers. Because women are frequently portrayed in advertising, popular literature and the mass media as shoppers, the practice of shopping is frequently characterised as a frivolity, a luxury and a waste of time. When the same activity is referred to as the acquisition of 'important' goods (such as stockmarket shares, machinery, cars, real estate and property) shopping is seen as a masculine occupation. As a consumer culture, the modern society is characterised as encouraging unbridled desire, exciting the emotions and senses, and encouraging new appetites. When these longings become addictions and are pathologised into uncontrollable and irrational forces, then they are associated metaphorically with the feminine. When they are deemed governable (that is, subject to 'masculine' control) these same impulses are described as adventurous, entrepreneurial and creative.

Fashion, although directed ostensibly at women in the modern era, has remained a male-dominated and economically driven activity. At the beginning of the twentieth century, male designers like Charles Frederick Worth (who only recently had entered the realm of feminine fashion) were in the process of transforming *haute couture* into an economically viable business venture. Even though the majority of fashion workers were women, it was believed that men were by nature *creators*, while women were merely *technicians* who performed the necessary but mundane tasks of transforming the ideas of male geniuses into actual clothes (Steele, 1992:122). Even those famous women couturiers, such as Coco Chanel, Elsa Schiaparelli and Madeleine Vionnet, who helped make Paris the fashion centre of the twentieth century, and whose success would seem to contradict generalisations about gender difference in the fashion industry, reveal in their autobiographies their sense of reliance on male support, financial and otherwise (ibid.:118–26).

Coco Chanel, in particular, had a colourful personal history that included working as an actor and a prostitute, although the veracity of this allegation is largely obscured by the mythology that still surrounds her. Steele suggests that Chanel entered the fashion business not as a result of her abilities as a designer but because it was commonplace in the *belle époque* for a wealthy man to 'set up his mistress in the hat business, so that she would be financially independent when he tired of her' (ibid.:119). Indeed, Salvador Dali recalled a conversation with Chanel in which she told him: 'I was able to open a high fashion shop because two gentlemen were outbidding each other for my hot little body' (ibid.).

While the success of fashion is implicated in the performative aspects of gender, it is also deeply dependent on assumptions about human nature. In Veblen's terms, fashion is the folly of the gullible. No rational, self-possessed human beings would allow themselves to be so easily exploited. In the early stages of mass consumerism (that is, in the first three decades of the twentieth century) it was widely assumed by manufacturers, retailers and advertisers that consumers were gullible and passive (see Cross, 1993). To some extent this came about as a result of the rationalisation of the workplace, for in this period individuals quickly become accustomed to being directed and subsumed by the needs of a restructuring and expanding capitalist enterprise. The new worker was believed to lack a sense of either personal independence or purpose in life. With such a mentality, individuals could be turned into perfect consumers of fashionable items; they simply treated as authoritative any suggestions of advertisers that they should own this or that commodity.

Another perspective on this matter is provided by critical debates on the nature of human needs, and how consumption signifies contradictory longings of essentially irrational individuals. The Marxist-oriented studies by Baudrillard (1981), Lefebvre (1971) and Debord (1970) argue this view with reference to those structural features by which capitalist economies dominate individual preferences and tastes. Although, for Baudrillard, human needs are not specifiable—that is, it cannot be said that we need this or that object—they can be understood nevertheless as desires for both 'difference' and social meaning (1988:45). When consumption is regarded as both a system of communication and a structure of exchange rather than a phenomenology of pleasure, then consumers act in accord with others. Consumption becomes part of the social bond. It does not express a natural need (or satisfaction or pleasure) but its opposite: it is a sign of how individuals live with arbitrary classifications.

Baudrillard maintains that we now inhabit a world which is totally different from any other, in so far as we live in less proximity to other human beings and in greater intimacy with technical and functional objects. Baudrillard writes: 'as the wolf-child becomes wolf by living among them, so are we becoming functional. We are living the period of the objects: that is, we live by their rhythm, according to their incessant cycles' (ibid.:29).

Implicit in this assessment of modern life is the great debate about human needs. Do humans have a need to consume? Is this need produced and sustained artificially? If there are different physiological and psychological needs, can we confidently separate and define them? Baudrillard sums up this troublesome debate by quoting the American economist J. K. Galbraith: 'man has become the object of science for man only since automobiles have become harder to sell than to manufacture' (ibid.:39). Needs are not separable and tied in some mysterious way to personal satisfaction: on the contrary, they exist as a 'force of consumption'. Even though the needs generated by a consumer ethic are largely false, they function effectively as strategies for maintaining the consumer economy (ibid.:43–4).

A mass consumption society does not necessarily result from new productive capacities. And individuals cannot be relied upon to absorb or to hold in balance these two structural forces—production and consumption. Rather, the play of advertising has a marked impact on consumer conduct, especially when it expounds new value systems and ideas. Some advertising accomplishes remarkable compressions of contradictory and unrelated materials, like those ads that characterise cigarettes as health adjuncts because they reduce stress or help with dieting (see Goldman, 1992; Marchand, 1985; Raymond Williams, 1980).

The fashion industries are closely serviced by advertising. Fashion is disseminated to its markets through media attention. It is intertwined with the modern temper of restlessness and openness to new experiences. Fashion serves to detach the grip of the past; it favours a loosening of tradition in order to allow people to respond more directly to immediate demands. The speed of the fashion cycle has been accelerating during the twentieth century. In the nineteenth century, styles of dress could take decades to change; in the twentieth century, new styles arrive before the old ones are discarded. Intensive capitalisation and the industrialisation of the garment industry have both contributed to this acceleration, as have consumer affluence, democratisation and the erosion of class barriers, and the faster flow of information through the media. It has resulted in an increased number of simultaneous fashions. Clothing styles for specific occasions—such as day or evening wear, town or country, business or leisure, home or office—have also influenced the simultaneity of fashions and increased the numbers in currency.

Herbert Blumer (1969), a sociologist from the American school of symbolic interactionism, sees fashion as an effective preparation for the demands of modern, urban life. Fashion encourages individuals to face the present, slough off the past, and immure themselves against the pull of tradition. Fashion reduces social anxiety by reconciling ambiguity and instability, which are the very ingredients of metropolitan life. It does this by embodying change and making it seem predictable. In this way, the instabilities and ambiguities of everyday life are read as expressions of various fashions and new social manners, and this perspective ameliorates much of the anxiety of the new. Blumer tacitly accepts the importance of goods in the social exchanges of modern life, and is neither suspicious nor wary of the practices which effect the consumption of fashionable commodities: for him, they are simply a given.

Blumer's position is not unlike that of material anthropologists, who have long understood the significance of goods in character-ising an individual's public persona. Irrespective of whether such goods originate in traditional sources or circulate rapidly in the currents of mass production, the relationship of individuals to their possessions is an important constituent of social life. Possessions cannot to be dismissed, overlooked or diminished by a moral assessment which denigrates goods as frivolities, especially if they are fashionable. Although goods function as social markers, they are also integral to the representations of the self. The choice, the purchase and the desire for specific items all speak to the individual as constituents of identity and social position. When the individual can specify the use of an acquired commodity in terms of personal desires which are separate from the uses conferred upon it by a marketing and advertising elite, then the object becomes personally significant. By imposing an idiosyncratic meaning on a commodity, we make it our own, and we are much less in danger of pursuing goods for their commodified and alienating qualities. When goods are fetishised by the label of fashion, their symbolic meanings mask their origins, and our desire for them is merely an example of the control that elite taste-makers can exert over us. In such instances, fashion becomes a form of oppression (Douglas and Isherwood, 1978; Daniel Miller, 1987).

The imagery of the fashion system has been dominated by *haute couture*, and the idea that appearances can be exclusive, privileged and individual. There are odd exceptions to this: the superiority of machine-manufactured over handmade goods is incontestable for basics such as lingerie, stockings, socks and undergarments. And blue jeans, beginning with Levi 501s, also exemplify how a mass-produced item may have distinct and attractive qualities (Leopold, 1992:115). None the less, the desirable image of being exclusive continues to permeate the fashion industries and to perpetuate the allure of designer-label products and 'hot' seasonable items. While a few goods such as jeans and work boots have filtered up through the fashion system in defiance of Veblen's theory of downward inflection, fashionability still resonates with the exclusivities of *haute couture*.

Fashion, however, is not propelled solely by economics. Although sophisticated manufacturing techniques have resulted in a global distribution system which enables fashion to rival the reach of the mass media, such economic efficiency and drive will not ensure its success. A highly technologised mass-manufacturer such as Benetton appears to have great control over the market. Yet the persistence of street-styles, retro, ethnic and local fashions indicates that the fashion business is not as directly and effectively manipulative of consumers as is often supposed.

Fashion persists in offering the allure of another life. It works best in a social climate which is saturated with commodities, each infused with promises of new sensations and new opportunities. The pluralism of fashion cannot be accounted for by the traditional theories of the trickle-down effect. Fashion reconciles the private and the social; it gives vent to personal impulses and spontaneous gestures through a general and publicly ritualised mode of consumption. In all these gestures, fashion eludes a purely economic explanation.

Fashion in the City

*The metropolis places emphasis on striving for the most indi-
vidual form of personal existence—regardless of whether it is
always correct or always successful.*

Georg Simmel

Alison Lurie describes city clothes as camouflage outfits because
they are the colours of stone, concrete and weak sunlight. They
are cut to make the rounded human form appear more rectangular.
Men's dress, in particular, is an assemblage of oblongs and stripes
which mirror the surrounding buildings. These clothes, Lurie
concludes, 'conceal city-dwellers from possible predators, or make
it easier for them to sneak up on their prey, or both . . .' (Lurie,
1992:103). Irrespective of whether she is serious or not, the point
remains that dress is treated here as an expression of the urban
streetscape.

In recent years, museums too have also acknowledged the
cultural significance of fashion by making it the subject of special
exhibitions. In 1993 the Australian National Gallery in Canberra
presented *Dressed to Kill: 100 Years of Fashion*. Beginning with
the work of Charles Worth, it included representative designs by
Jeanne Lanvin, Paco Rabanne, Zandra Rhodes, Rei Kawakubo,
Christian Lacroix and many others, among them the once renegade
but now establishment designer Vivienne Westwood. Coinciden-
tally the National Gallery of Victoria put on *From Worth to Dior,*

a much smaller exhibition but similar in its concentration on the designer as artist. In 1994 the Powerhouse in Sydney focused on the brilliance of Christian Dior as a fashion designer in an exhibition subtitled *The Magic of Fashion*. In London, over the 1994–95 holiday period, the Victoria and Albert Museum presented *Streetstyle, From Sidewalk to Catwalk, 1940 to Tomorrow,* which was curated by the popular media anthropologist Ted Polhemus. It classified youth culture and style-tribes through clothes dating from post-World War II. Beginning with 1940s zoot suits from New York's Harlem, and extending to the eclecticism of the 1990s (New Age traveller, rocker, rasta, punk, biker, surfer, rockabilly, goth and hipster), the exhibition promised to explain the phenomenon of street-style.

The confluence of interests in fashion from museums, department stores and advertising agencies has firmly established it as a spectacle to be analysed like any other aesthetic formation. The dominant assumption in the *Streetstyle* exhibition is that clothing styles are 'thick' with anthropologically significant meanings which reveal the political and social positions of those who adopt them. To choose a particular garment, hair-style or make-up is simultaneously to express a particular subcultural world-view. Polhemus goes further in positing that clothes can represent complex ideas, attitudes and values, and that direct connections are discernible between the visibility of one's appearance and the invisibility of one's political and aesthetic values (1994:15). Dress, he points out, is capable of signalling either a concern for environmental issues (in, say, hippie wear) or political nihilism and anarchy, as in punk wear: 'The Punks' black leather, fetishistic garments, studs and Crazy Colour hairstyles indicate a nihilism, an aggressive stance and a delight in artifice and deliberate perversity' (ibid.). Dress can signify any position on the political spectrum.

To discern character or politics in appearances is not a new phenomenon. As modern societies began to eliminate sumptuary laws and rigid codes of dress, opportunities arose for individuals to construct or fashion themselves as they pleased. Such flexibility of self-representation, which has been a driving force in the rapid development of the fashion industries, is also a defining feature of modernity. The modern era is marked by constant innovation and the pursuit of novelty in technical, political, social and aesthetic arenas. By emphasising the seductiveness of the new and deriding the past, fashion becomes synonymous with the urban and the modern. As Douglas Kellner states:

> fashion is a constituent feature of modernity, interpreted as an era of history marked by perpetual innovation, by the destruction of the old and the creation of the new. Fashion itself is predicated on producing ever new tastes, artifacts, and practices. Fashion perpetuates a restless, modern personality, always seeking what is new and admired, while avoiding what is old and passé. Fashion and modernity go hand in hand to produce modern personalities. (1994:161)

In particular, this has permitted 'celebrity' to impinge directly on the development of individual identities:

> Michael Jackson, Prince, Boy George, and other rock groups undermined traditional gender divisions and promoted polymorphic sexuality. Cyndi Lauper reveled in offbeat kookiness, and Pee Wee Herman engaged in silly and infantile behavior . . . Throwing off decades of cool sophistication, maturity, respectability, and taste, Pee Wee made it OK to be silly and weird, or at least different. (ibid.:162)

According to Kellner, one of the strongest influences on urban identity has been Madonna:

> Madonna's constant change of fashion, image, and identity promoted experimentation and the creation of one's own style and identity. Her sometimes dramatic shifts in identity suggested that identity was a construct, that it was something that one produced and could be modified at will. The way Madonna deployed fashion in the construction of her identity made it clear that one's appearance and image helps produce what one is, or least how one is perceived . . . Madonna's hair changed from dirty blonde to platinum blonde, to black, brunette, redhead, and multifarious variations thereof. Her body changed from soft and sensuous to glamorous and svelte to

hard and muscular sex machine to futuristic technobody. Her clothes and fashion changed from flashy trash to haute couture to far-out technoculture to lesbian S & M fashion to postmodern pastiche of all and every fashion style. (ibid.:162–3)

The interweave of identity with geography—or more accurately, topography—was observed in the early years of the twentieth century by Georg Simmel, who argued that the rapid growth of city centres had changed the way people related to one another. Simmel (1950:409–24) describes the city as a noisy, highly stimulating background against which people attempt to transact their business and to maintain a private life. The intrusive background, however, affects the individual's sense of identity and singularity, as well as the postures and demeanour regarded as appropriate in the public arena. The city changes the way people interrelate by affecting how they see both themselves (as diminutive and undistinguished) and others (as potentially affronting and the source of unanticipated demands). In response to the pressures of metropolitan life, individuals assume a blasé attitude, that is, a sense of social detachment which provides a buffer between themselves and the rush of the everyday. By also cultivating a show of singularity or individualism through status symbols such as fashionability, they attempt to ameliorate that loss of identity and sense of submergence which the city engenders.

In the urban context described by Simmel, fashion serves to protect individuals from a sense of being ground-down, levelled out and overwhelmed by the overarching socio-technological mechanism that is the metropolis. Simmel argues that the city embodies a total objectification of culture. Consequently, in order to survive in this context, people struggle toward extreme subjectivism, performing and asserting themselves so as to recuperate a sense of individuality in an environment marked by indifference. Such displays, however, cannot succeed in marking the individual as truly different. To be different in the city is to be unreadable to others, and hence to be submerged and invisible. The aim of being fashionable is to be individualistic within a shared code, since individuals can look distinctive only within a restricted aesthetic. When they purchase fashionable goods that will distinguish them, they do so only from a range of goods already understood to be valuable. To succeed in being fashionable, then, involves having specific knowledge about the value of goods. It is not sufficient to desire goods simply because of their utility. Fashion goods have more symbolic and cultural value than use-value, and as such they constitute a new type of commodity. Much of their significance comes from their visibility and prominence on the street.

The street can be a mysterious place. Physically a passageway that gives direction, it is a topographical feature which carves up every city into precincts with distinctive characteristics. The street is a boundary and a margin; as a route which leads somewhere it suggests inherent purpose. But for all their simplicity, these physical features generate conceptual ambiguity. Because direction, purpose, boundaries and categories are cornerstones of the post-structural reconstruction, the street can be seen as an effective metaphor expressing the concerns of the times. And when individuals use the street in a self-conscious manner, then these covert ambiguities are exploited, as in the ubiquitous wearing of T-shirts smothered in logos of the most banal nature, such as 'G'Day Australia', 'Coca-Cola', or 'The Hard Rock Cafe'. It is always possible (but never unequivocally so) that these familiar surfaces are bracketed for purposes of irony and satire. Street-wear, in these instances, can be a platform for enunciating messages that invite aesthetic challenge and social scrutiny.

Street-styles often perform as declarations of serious social causes. Various utopian rebels and social reformers have used costume and dress styles as public announcements of alternative outlooks (Luck, 1992; Ribeiro, 1992). In early industrial France, groups such as Les Barbus, the Saint-Simonians and Les Jeunes France used miscellaneous styles of appearance to signify their disavowal of the mainstream: classical togas, red waistcoats, brightly coloured trousers and hats, long hair and beards, and loose, wet negligees. Counter-cultural dress has long been a device for publicising social malaise and political critique, in much the same way that conventional dress codes signify an acceptance of the status quo.

However, just as Alison Lurie's superficial reading of city clothes is more amusing than insightful, the interpretation of any fashion style, counter-cultural or otherwise, can be equally limited because the visual nature of appearances cannot be confined to specific messages. Radical politics are more varied and subtle than any T-shirt display can acknowledge. Even so, given the scepticism provoked by interpretations of fashion and style, it is ironic that a desire to read the obvious as if it were self-revealing should endure. This is exemplified in the persistent use of fashion hierarchies to reflect class, status and conventionality, even when the mutual cannibalisation of fashions from every position on the political spectrum continues as part of the sartorial cycle. For instance, when street-stylists have lost the ability to shock, and the most audacious styles have become elements in mainstream costuming (such as the absorption of S/M fetish wear into *haute couture*, and the prevalence of cross-dressing on international fashion house catwalks), a belief still endures in the authenticity of appearances, and in the ability of the costumed body to speak and act as both a manifesto of rebellion and a mirror to convention.

All fashions remain ambivalent because the question of whether they are meant to be confrontational or affirmational is indeterminate. When the *haute couture* gown is paraded in drag, its original value is hard to discern: this is the point made by Diane Arbus's photography (Shloss, 1994). The same point is made by Jennie Livingston in her documentary film, *Paris Is Burning*, which records the drag balls attended by African-American and Latino men in New York City and Harlem. Fashion styles selected mainly from the straight 'white' world are here performed and judged, and the categories of costumes include Ivy League, executive, the military look, high drag feminine and butch queen. Judith Butler (1993:129) enquires after the meaning of these performances: do they subvert the norm or re-idealise it, and how does an onlooker know when the appearance coincides with what it means? When other styles are imitated, it is questionable whether the resultant faux-fashion is to be understood as fakery or as failure. Does faux-fashion undercut or concretise the fashion hierarchy (Ross, 1994:286)? When casual and street-wear were first smothered in logos they could be read as mockery of the fashion label; as the inscriptions and insignia on such items of clothing became more prominent, the iconoclasm lost its impact. Parading the label no longer exposed the middle-class fetish of buying symbolic power; it merely announced a new consumer aesthetic.

Take the example of the sports cap. Was it ever used only to indicate support for a particular football, baseball or basketball team? Has its recent appropriation by ethnic groups subverted its meaning? Is its meaning anything more than globalised Americanicity? Is it worn for its aesthetic appeal on account of its bright colours and design, or as a sign of club membership or class affiliation (as the traditional hat of farmers, truck-drivers and factory workers)? The sports cap has always been prominent in rural America, but in the city, and especially when worn back to front, it has recently become a sign of social crisis (ibid.:288). As soon as it assumes this meaning, the reversed cap becomes part of middle-class fashion paraphernalia. The fashion Moloch has absorbed yet another attempt at oppositional dress. Much the same can be said of hair-styles. The shaved head may allude to a military-style puritanism, parody the institutionalised look or (as in the Comme des Garçons example) gesture ambivalently toward the victims of war. Body-piercing and tattooing can be seen to recuperate the practices of 'primitive' peoples, but they can also evoke a technoculture in which semi-criminalised individuals are identified by numbers and body-brandings. (ibid.:295–6)

Those constant renovations in fashion which attempt to express subcultural variations are also, according to Polhemus, expressions of tribal pedigrees. This is particularly apparent in urban settings, where the assertion of identity is felt to be urgent. Body-marking and traditional costumes make equivalent claims to identity. An inherent feature of human sociality, notes Polhemus, is the securing of a social identity:

the tribal imperative is and always will be a fundamental part of human nature. Like our most distant ancestors we feel alienated and purposeless when we do not experience this sense of belonging and comradeship. It is no coincidence that the decline of traditional social groupings, which has intensified so markedly since the Second World War precisely parallels the rise of a new type of social group, the *styletribe*. Hipsters, Teddy Boys, Mods, Rockers and so forth arose to satisfy that need for a sense of community and common purpose which is so lacking in modern life. (1994:14)

The proliferation of contemporary styles in the west is to be expected because of the growth in the public domain. The street is where modern classifications and claims to identity are now staged. The urban street has become a metaphor for modern social life; it is at once 'a dead end—the place to go when you aren't old enough or rich enough to get in somewhere' and an exciting alternative which is 'seductive for many who could be elsewhere' (ibid.:7). The street represents the 'real thing'; it is the authentic urban experience, the inescapable fact at the end of the road, both literally and figuratively.

Urban fashion is a means of acquiring multiple lives. It works best in a social climate saturated with commodities, each of which is infused with promises of new sensations and new opportunities. The transformative properties of fashion are embedded in every new purchase (DeLibero, 1994:46). Fashion is a short cut that enables consumers to enter another identity, to join a subculture and to insulate themselves from contamination by other styles. Dick Hebdige calls fashion goods 'weapons of exclusion' (1988:110).

W. F. Haug prefers the phrase 'aesthetic innovation' to fashion when describing how the marketing technique of 'out with the old, in with the new' continues to work so effectively (1986:41–2). What propels the consumer ethic is the idea that aesthetics are being developed or renovated as continuously as essential goods are being restyled. The inherent dynamism of fashion is represented as a 'natural' mechanism whereby all objects are forever changing, becoming outdated, being devalued and in need of replacement. This emphasis on the aesthetic innovation of goods prevents us from recognising the importance of economic buoyancy as the submerged force in fashion.

The crowded city, where different people pursue different purposes, is a constant reminder of the need for change, which thus makes fashion seem a natural feature of the environment.

The emphasis that city life gives to appearances concentrates attention on the fashionable. Fashion is a disciplinary power in Foucault's sense, in that it coerces the body to shape and rearrange itself in accordance with ever-shifting social expectations. The skills required to diet, to apply facial cosmetics, to arrange clothes and to wear ornamentation are in the service of aesthetic innovations that continually reinvent our identities. Foucault's notion of the docile body shows how elements of a fashionable lifestyle—which include the urban habits of reading fashion magazines, engaging in body-sculpting practices such as dieting, gym work-outs, cosmetic surgery and periodic internments at health and fat farms—are techniques for transforming the body into a commodity. The body becomes a site of aesthetic innovation, much like the family car, and subject to periodic upgrading. To redesign the look of a commodity is to give it a new lease of life, specifically by submerging its use-value into its appearance-value. 'Looking good' adds value: those who cannot achieve the fashionable 'look' fail the appearance test, and their social status declines. Urban life, which constantly exposes everybody to the scrutiny of strangers, emphasises the need to monitor and to update one's self-performance.

This imperative to be self-conscious is a distinguishing feature of the modern city, and is reflected in the various guises one can assume. So naturalised is the idea that each of us plays multiple roles and has various styles of appearance that the Mattel toy manufacturers use it in their advertising campaign to sell their most popular item, the Barbie doll. Ingeborg O'Sickey (1994) discusses how Barbie dolls function to induct young girls into accepting fashionability as a condition of modern, urban life by introducing them to various beauty practices and style alternatives. Barbie dolls represent one of those territories in which the power that naturalises fashion for women is made popular and acceptable. Each Barbie doll is segmentable into constituent personae (through changes of outfits) and parts (through attention to lips, hair, arms, legs, finger-nails and so on). The phenomenal success of Barbie dolls has promoted the illusion that the eleven-and-a-half-inch model is an actual celebrity who personifies eternal youth. She is the modern woman—corporate member, party girl, girlfriend and fashion follower. Barbie dolls embody the connections between commodities (gendered feminine in the economy that manipulates them) and women (commodified as products of the fashion industry).

If personal identity is one of the problems of modernity, then it is equally true that the fashion industries are deeply implicated in the manufacture of 'personality'. When the youth fashion houses like Stüssy and Benetton invent and reinvent global tribe membership, they are formulating a potent mix of eco-politics, post-urban lifestyle and old-fashioned capitalism. It is too simple to explain their successes by saying that human beings have a chronic need to belong, or by referring to clever marketing and consumer exploitation. In many ways they encapsulate the problems inherent in attempts to account for the circulation of the fashionable. They redefine the quest after a fashion as the contemporary quandary of explaining how society ever came to be possible. The analysis of fashion, as an economic, psychological, historical and social phenomenon, can take this enquiry even further.

Bibliography

Ackroyd, Peter (1979) *Dressing Up*, London: Thames and Hudson
Age, Extra, 19 November 1994, p. 16
Appadurai, Arjun (ed.) (1986) *The Social Life of Things: Commodities in Cultural Perspective*, Cambridge: Cambridge University Press
—— (1990) 'Disjuncture and Difference in the Global Cultural Economy', *Public Culture* 2, 2, Fall, pp. 1–24
Ash, Juliet (1992) 'Philosophy on the Catwalk: The Making and Wearing of Vivienne Westwood's Clothes' in Wilson and Ash (eds) *Chic Thrills*, pp. 167–85
Bacon, Francis (1974) *The Advancement of Learning and New Atlantis*, Oxford: Clarendon Press [1627]
Barthes, Roland (1985) *The Fashion System*, New York: Jonathan Cape [1967]
Bartky, Sandra (1988) 'Foucault, Femininity, and the Modernization of Patriarchal Power' in Irene Diamond and Lee Quinby (eds) *Feminism and Foucault*, Boston: Northeastern University Press, pp. 61–86
Baudrillard, Jean (1981) *For a Critique of the Political Economy of the Sign*, St Louis, Missouri: Telos Press [1972]
—— (1988) *Selected Writings*, Oxford: Polity
—— (1990) *Revenge of the Crystal,* Sydney: Pluto Press and Power Institute
—— (1993) *Symbolic Exchange and Death*, London: Sage [1976]

Bell, Quentin (1976) *Of Human Finery*, London: Hogarth Press [1947]

Benstock, Shari and Suzanne Ferriss (eds) (1994) *On Fashion*, New Brunswick, New Jersey: Rutgers University Press

Bergler, Edmund (1987) *Fashion and the Unconscious*, New York: Robert Brunner [1953]

Blumer, Herbert (1969) 'Fashion: From Class Differentiation to Collective Selection', *Sociological Quarterly* 10, pp. 275–91

Bordo, Susan (1993) '"Material Girl": The Effacements of Postmodern Culture' in Cathy Schwichtenberg (ed.) *The Madonna Connection*, Sydney: Allen and Unwin, pp. 265–90

Bourdieu, Pierre (1984) *Distinction: A Social Critique of the Judgment of Taste*, Cambridge, Massachusetts: Harvard University Press [1979]

Bowlby, Rachel (1985) *Just Looking: Consumer Culture in Dreiser, Gissing and Zola*, London: Methuen

—— (1993) *Shopping with Freud*, London: Routledge

Braudel, Fernand (1973) *Capitalism and Material Life 1400–1800*, New York: Harper and Row [1967]

Brookes, Rosetta (1992) 'Fashion Photography: The Double-Page Spread: Helmut Newton, Guy Bourdin and Deborah Turbeville' in Wilson and Ash (eds) *Chic Thrills*, pp. 17–24

Burgin, Victor, James Donald and Cora Kaplan (eds) (1986) *Formations of Fantasy*, London: Routledge

Butler, Judith (1993) *Bodies that Matter: On the Discursive Limits of "Sex"*, New York: Routledge

Camhi, Leslie (1993) 'Stealing Femininity: Department Store Kleptomania as Sexual Disorder', *differences* 5, 1, pp. 26–50

Carlyle, Thomas (1831) *Sartor Resartus: The Life and Opinions of Herr Teufelsdröckh*, London: Curwen Press

Chapman, Rowena and Jonathan Rutherford (eds) (1988) *Male Order: Unwrapping Masculinity*, London: Lawrence and Wishart

Chenoune, Farid (1993) *A History of Men's Fashion*, London: Flammarion Thames and Hudson

Cixous, Hélène (1994) 'Sonia Rykiel in Translation' in Benstock and Ferriss (eds) *On Fashion*, pp. 95–9

Coleridge, Nicholas (1988) *The Fashion Conspiracy*, London: William Heinemann

Coward, Rosalind (1984) *Female Desires: How They Are Sought, Bought and Packaged*, London: Paladin

Craik, Jennifer (1994) *The Face of Fashion*, London: Routledge

Cross, Gary (1993) *Time & Money: The Making of Consumer Culture*, London: Routledge

Csikszentmihalyi, Mihaly and Eugene Rochberg-Halton (1981) *The Meaning of Things: Domestic Symbols and the Self*, Cambridge: Cambridge University Press

Davenport, Millia (1952) *A History of Costume*, London: Thames and Hudson [1948]

Davis, Fred (1992) *Fashion, Culture, and Identity*, Chicago: University of Chicago Press

de Certeau, Michel (1984) *The Practices of Everyday Life*, Berkeley, California: University of California Press

Debord, Guy (1970) *The Society of the Spectacle*, Detroit: Black and Red [1967]

DeLibero, Linda (1994) 'This Year's Girl: A Personal/Critical History of Twiggy' in Benstock and Ferriss (eds) *On Fashion*, pp. 41–58

Douglas, Mary (1966) *Purity and Danger*, London: Routledge and Kegan Paul

—— (1973) *Natural Symbols*, Middlesex: Penguin

Douglas, Mary and Baron Isherwood (1978) *The World of Goods: Towards an Anthropology of Consumption*, Middlesex: Penguin

du Plessix Gray, Francine (1981) 'The Escape from Fashion', *Dial* 2, 9, pp. 43–7

Eco, Umberto (1986) 'Lumbar Thoughts' in *Faith In Fakes*, London: Secker and Warburg, pp. 191–5

Elias, Norbert (1978) *The Civilizing Process*, New York: Urizen [1939]

—— (1983) *The Court Society*, Oxford: Blackwell [1969]

Evans, Caroline and Minna Thornton (1989) *Women and Fashion*, London: Quartet

Ewen, Stuart and Elizabeth Ewen (1982) *Channels of Desire: Mass Images and the Shaping of American Consciousness*, New York: McGraw-Hill

Featherstone, Mike (1991) *Consumer Culture and Postmodernism*, London: Sage

Finch, Casey (1991) '"Hooked and Buttoned Together": Victorian Underwear and Representations of the Female Form', *Victorian Studies* 34, 3, pp. 337–63

Finkelstein, Joanne (1991) *The Fashioned Self*, Oxford: Polity

Flügel, John Carl (1930) *The Psychology of Clothes*, London: Hogarth

Foucault, Michel (1977) *Discipline and Punish*, London: Allen Lane

Fox-Genovese, Elisabeth (1978) 'Yves Saint Laurent's Peasant Revolution', *Marxist Perspectives* 1, 2, pp. 58–93

Fuss, Diana (1992) 'Fashion and the Homospectatorial Look', *Critical Inquiry* 18, pp. 713–37

Gaines, Jane (1990) 'Costume and Narrative: How Dress Tells the Woman's Story' in Gaines and Herzog (eds) *Fabrications*, pp. 180–211

Gaines, Jane and Charlotte Herzog (eds) (1990) *Fabrications: Costume and the Female Body*, London: Routledge

Garber, Marjorie (1992) *Vested Interests: Cross-Dressing and Cultural Anxiety*, New York: Routledge

Gardner, Carl and Julie Sheppard (1989) *Consuming Passion: The Rise of Retail Culture*, London: Unwin Hyman

Giroux, Henry (1993–94) 'Consuming Social Change: The "United Colors of Benetton"', *Cultural Critique* 26, Winter, pp. 5–32

Goldman, Robert (1992) *Reading Ads Socially*, London: Routledge

Gottdiener, Mark (1977) 'Unisex Fashion and Gender Role Change', *Semiotic Scene* 1, 3, pp. 13–37

Griggers, Cathy (1990) 'A Certain Tension in the Visual/Cultural Field: Helmut Newton, Deborah Turbeville and the VOGUE Fashion Layout', *differences* 2, 2, pp. 76–104

Hansen, Joseph and Evelyn Reed (1986) *Cosmetics, Fashion and the Exploitation of Women*, New York: Pathfinder Press

Haug, Wolfgang Fritz (1986) *Commodity Aesthetics*, Oxford: Polity [1971]

Hebdige, Dick (1979) *Subculture: The Meaning of Style*, London: Methuen

—— (1988) *Hiding in the Light: On Images and Things*, London: Routledge

—— (1993) 'A Report from the Western Front: Postmodernism and the "Politics" of Style' in Chris Jenks (ed.) *Cultural Reproduction*, New York: Routledge, pp. 69–103

Hollander, Anne (1980) *Seeing Through Clothes*, New York: Avon
—— (1994) *Sex and Suits*, New York: Knopf
Hume, Marion (1995) 'Fashion: A History of Controversy on the Catwalk', *Independent* [newspaper], 10 February
Huxley, Aldous (1932) *Brave New World*, London: Chatto and Windus
Jameson, Fredric (1990) *Postmodernism, or The Cultural Logic of Late Capitalism*, Durham, North Carolina: Duke University Press
Kassarjian, Harold H. and Thomas S. Robertson (eds) (1985) *Handbook of Consumer Behavior*, New Brunswick, New Jersey: Prentice-Hall
Kellner, Douglas (1994) 'Madonna, Fashion, Identity' in Benstock and Ferriss (eds) *On Fashion*, pp. 159–82
Kennedy, Fraser (1985) *The Fashionable Mind*, Boston: David Godine
König, René (1973) *The Restless Image: A Sociology of Fashion*, London: Allen and Unwin
Kunzle, David (1982) *Fashion and Fetishism: A Social History of the Corset, Tight-Lacing and Other Forms of Body-Sculpture in the West*, Totowa, New Jersey: Rowman and Littlefield
Laver, James (1937) *Taste and Fashion*, London: George Harrap
—— (1969a) *A Concise History of Costume*, London: Thames and Hudson
—— (1969b) *Modesty in Dress*, London: Heinemann
Leach, Edmund (1958) 'Magical Hair', *Journal of the Royal Anthropological Institute* 88, 2, pp. 147–64
Leaska, Mitchell and John Phillips (1989) *Violet to Vita: The Letters of Violet Trefusis to Vita Sackville-West 1910–21*, London: Methuen
Lefebvre, Henri (1971) *Everyday Life in the Modern World*, New York: Harper Torch Books [1968]
Leong, Roger (1993) *Dressed to Kill: 100 Years of Fashion*, Canberra: National Gallery of Australia
Leopold, Ellen (1992) 'The Manufacture of the Fashion System' in Wilson and Ash (eds) *Chic Thrills*, pp. 101–16
Lévi-Strauss, Claude (1972) *The Savage Mind*, London: Weidenfeld and Nicolson [1966]

Lipovetsky, Gilles (1994) *The Empire of Fashion: Dressing Modern Democracy*, Princeton, New Jersey: Princeton University Press [1987]

Livingston, Jennie (dir.) (1990) *Paris Is Burning*, Premium Films, USA

Luck, Kate (1992) 'Trouble in Eden, Trouble with Eve' in Wilson and Ash (eds) *Chic Thrills*, pp. 200–12

Lunt, Peter and Sonia Livingstone (1992) *Mass Consumption and Personal Identity*, Buckingham, Philadelphia: Open University Press

Lurie, Alison (1992) *The Language of Clothes*, London: Bloomsbury [1981]

McCracken, Grant (1988) *Culture and Consumption*, Bloomington: Indiana University Press

McKendrick, Neil, John Brewer and J. H. Plumb (1982) *The Birth of a Consumer Society*, London: Europa

McRobbie, Angela (ed.) (1988) *Zoot Suits and Second-Hand Dresses: An Anthology of Fashion and Music*, London: Unwin Hyman

Marchand, Roland (1985) *Advertising: The American Dream 1920–1940*, Berkeley, California: University of California Press

Maynard, Margaret (1994) *Fashioned From Penury: Dress as Cultural Practice in Colonial Australia*, Cambridge: Cambridge University Press

Miller, Daniel (1987) *Material Culture and Mass Consumption*, Oxford: Blackwell

Miller, Michael (1981) *The Bon Marché: Bourgeois Culture and the Department Store 1869–1920*, Princeton, New Jersey: Princeton University Press

Mitchell, Louise et al. (1994) *Christian Dior: The Magic of Fashion*, Sydney: Powerhouse Museum

Moers, Ellen (1960) *The Dandy: Brummell to Beerbohm*, Lincoln: University of Nebraska Press

Molloy, John (1975) *Dress for Success*, New York: Warner Books

—— (1977) *The Woman's Dress for Success Book*, New York: Warner Books

More, Thomas (1965) *Utopia*, Middlesex: Penguin [1516]

Morris, William (1970) *News from Nowhere*, Boston: Routledge and Kegan Paul [1891]

Mukerji, Chandra (1983) *From Graven Images: Patterns of Modern Materialism*, New York: Columbia University Press

Nava, Mica (1981) 'Consumerism and its Contradictions', *Cultural Studies* 1, 2, pp. 204–10

Nixon, Sean (1992) 'Have You Got the Look? Masculinities and Shopping Spectacle' in Shields (ed.) *Lifestyle Shopping*, pp. 149–69

O'Sickey, Ingeborg (1994) 'Barbie Magazine and the Aesthetic Commodification of Girls' Bodies' in Benstock and Ferriss (eds) *On Fashion*, pp. 21–40

Packard, Vance (1957) *The Hidden Persuaders*, Middlesex: Penguin

Partington, Angela (1992) 'Popular Fashion and Working-Class Affluence' in Wilson and Ash (eds) *Chic Thrills*, pp. 145–61

Perrot, Philippe (1994) *Fashioning The Bourgeoisie: A History of Clothing in the Nineteenth Century*, Princeton, New Jersey: Princeton University Press [1981]

Poggioli, Renato (1968) *The Theory of the Avant-Garde*, Cambridge, Massachusetts: Belknap [1962]

Polhemus, Ted (1994) *Streetstyle: From Sidewalk to Catwalk*, London: Thames and Hudson

Polhemus, Ted and Lynn Proctor (1978) *Fashion and Anti-Fashion*, London: Thames and Hudson

Rabine, Leslie (1994) 'A Woman's Two Bodies: Fashion Magazines, Consumerism, and Feminism' in Benstock and Ferriss (eds) *On Fashion*, pp. 59–75

Radway, Janice (1984) *Reading the Romance*, London: Verso

Reekie, Gail (1992) 'Changes in the Adamless Eden: The Spatial and Sexual Transformation of a Brisbane Department Store 1930–90' in Shields (ed.) *Lifestyle Shopping*, pp. 170–94

—— (1993) *Temptations: Sex, Selling and the Department Store*, Sydney: Allen and Unwin

Ribeiro, Aileen (1986) *Dress and Morality*, London: Batsford

—— (1992) 'Utopian Dress' in Wilson and Ash (eds) *Chic Thrills*, pp. 225–37

Roberts, Hélène (1977) 'The Exquisite Slave: The Role of Clothes in the Making of the Victorian Woman', *Signs* 2, 3, pp. 554–69

Rolley, Katrina (1990) 'Cutting a Dash: The Dress of Radclyffe Hall and Una Troubridge', *Feminist Review* 35, pp. 54–66

—— (1992) 'Love, Desire and the Pursuit of the Whole: Dress and the Lesbian Couple' in Wilson and Ash (eds) *Chic Thrills*, pp. 30–9

Ross, Andrew (1994) 'Tribalism in Effect' in Benstock and Ferriss (eds) *On Fashion*, pp. 284–99

Rykiel, Sonia (1994) 'From *Celebration*' in Benstock and Ferriss (eds) *On Fashion*, pp. 100–8

Sahlins, Marshall (1976) *Culture and Practical Reason*, Chicago: University of Chicago Press

Schilder, Paul (1935) *The Image and Appearance of the Human Body: Studies of the Constructive Energies in the Psyche*, New York: International Universities Press

Shields, Rob (ed.) (1992) *Lifestyle Shopping: The Subjectivity of Consumption*, London: Routledge

Shloss, Carol (1994) 'Off the (W)rack: Fashion and Pain in the Work of Diane Arbus' in Benstock and Ferriss (eds) *On Fashion*, pp. 111–24

Silverman, Kaja (1986) 'Fragments of a Fashionable Discourse' in Tania Modleski (ed.) *Studies in Entertainment: Critical Approaches to Mass Culture*, Bloomington: University of Indiana Press, pp. 139–52

Simmel, Georg (1950) 'Adornment' in *The Sociology of Georg Simmel*, New York: Free Press, pp. 338–44

—— (1971) *On Individuality and Social Forms*, Chicago: University of Chicago Press, Chicago

—— (1971a) 'Fashion' in Simmel *On Individuality and Social Forms*, pp. 294–323 [1904]

—— (1971b) 'The Metropolis and Mental Life' in Simmel *On Individuality and Social Forms*, pp. 324–39 [1903]

—— (1978) *The Philosophy of Money*, London: Routledge, Kegan and Paul

Sontag, Susan (1966) 'Notes on Camp' in *Against Interpretation*, New York: Farrar, Straus and Giroux

Spencer, Neil (1992) 'Menswear in the 1980s: Revolt into Conformity' in Wilson and Ash (eds) *Chic Thrills*, pp. 40–8

Steele, Valerie (1985) *Fashion and Eroticism: Ideals of Feminine Beauty from the Victorian Era to the Jazz Age*, Oxford: Oxford University Press

—— (1988) *Paris Fashion: A Cultural History*, Oxford: Oxford University Press

—— (1992) 'Chanel in Context' in Wilson and Ash (eds) *Chic Thrills*, pp. 118–26

Stone, Gregory (1954) 'City Shoppers and Urban Identification: Observations on the Social Psychology of City Life', *American Journal of Sociology* 60, pp. 36–45

Swanson, Gillian (1994) '"Drunk with the Glitter": Consuming Spaces and Sexual Geographies' in Sophie Watson and Kathy Gibson (eds) *Postmodern Cities and Spaces*, Oxford: Blackwell, pp. 80–98

Taylor, Lou (1992) 'Paris Couture 1940–1944' in Wilson and Ash (eds) *Chic Thrills*, pp. 127–44.

Triggs, Teal (1992) 'Framing Masculinity: Herb Ritts, Bruce Weber and the Body Perfect' in Wilson and Ash (eds) *Chic Thrills*, pp. 25–9

Turim, Maureen (1990) 'Designing Women: The Emergence of the New Sweetheart Line' in Gaines and Herzog (eds) *Fabrications*, pp. 212–28

Veblen, Thorstein (1899) *A Theory of the Leisure Class*, New York: American Classics

von Boehn, Max (1932) *Modes and Manners*, 4 vols, New York: Benjamin Blom

Wells, H. G. (1922) *A Modern Utopia*, London: Nelson [1905]

Williams, Raymond (1980) 'Advertising: The Magic System' in *Problems in Materialism and Culture*, London: Verso

Williams, Rosalind (1982) *Dream Worlds: Mass Consumption in Late Nineteenth-Century France*, Berkeley, California: University of California Press

Wilson, Elizabeth (1985) *Adorned in Dreams: Fashion and Modernity*, London: Virago

—— (1990) 'Deviant Dress', *Feminist Review* 35, pp. 67–74

—— (1992) 'Fashion and the Postmodern Body' in Wilson and Ash (eds) *Chic Thrills*, pp. 3–16

Wilson, Elizabeth and Juliet Ash (eds) (1992) *Chic Thrills*, Berkeley, California: University of California Press

Wilson, Elizabeth and Laurie Taylor (1989) *Through the Looking Glass*, London: BBC Books

Wright, Lee (1992) 'Outgrown Clothes for Grown-Up People: Constructing a Theory of Fashion' in Wilson and Ash (eds) *Chic Thrills*, pp. 49–57

Yanowitch, Lee (1995a) 'Designer Withdraws Pyjamas after Jews Protest', Reuters News Service, 7 February

—— (1995b) 'Pyjama Gaffe Shakes Fashion World into Reality', Reuters News Service, 20 February

Zola, Émile (1957) *Ladies' Delight*, London: John Calder [1883]

Index

Other Interpretations titles available from Melbourne University Press:

After Mabo
Interpreting indigenous traditions
TIM ROWSE

Many non-Aboriginal Australians, sensitive to the fact that their nation came into existence through the conquest and dispossession of indigenous peoples, continue to seek ways of righting historical wrongs. A significant stage was reached in the High Court's so-called Mabo decision of June 1992, which recognised a 'native right in land'. Tim Rowse draws on history, political science, anthropology, cultural studies, ecology and archaeology to critique non-Aboriginal ways of perceiving Aboriginality. He focuses on the moral and legal traditions of settlers and indigenous peoples, their different attitudes towards the environment, the institutional heritage of 'Aboriginal welfare', tensions between indigenous cultures and indigenous politics, and the representation of Aboriginal identities by Aboriginal writers.

> 'a stylish and shrewd book . . . should be read by all who try to follow Mabo' Barry Hill, Age

The Body in the Text
ANNE CRANNY-FRANCIS

Male/female, white/black, mind/body: these fundamental distinctions, based on the way we see ourselves and others, face irrevocable breakdown as we stand on the edge of revolutions in artificial intelligence, robotics and genetic engineering. Cranny-Francis gives a lucid and stylish introduction to the ways in which the body is represented in our culture. Her clear, considered analysis shows how these representations are used as critiques of contemporary society by writers on gender, sexuality, race and class, and describes how these representations have changed the relationships between our understandings of the body and the ways in which we live and think about our world.

Debating Derrida
NIALL LUCY

'There is nothing outside the text.' Possibly no single statement has caused such a storm in critical theory as this famous observation by the French philosopher, Jacques Derrida. While it is often misunderstood as meaning that nothing is real, *Debating Derrida* demonstrates that Derrida's philosophy does not lack political conviction.

Niall Lucy examines three key terms—text, writing and *différance*—as they are used in three famous debates: Derrida's disputes over speech-acts with John R. Searle, over discourse with Michel Foucault and over apartheid. Lucy also takes up the issue of Derrida's relationship to postmodernism. *Debating*

Derrida decisively shows that instead of disagreeing with Derrida, we should rather be defending him.

A Foucault Primer
Discourse, power and the subject
ALEC MCHOUL AND WENDY GRACE

The French historian and philosopher, Michel Foucault, has had a profound influence on scholars in the humanities and social sciences for the last three decades. This book is designed for those attempting to come to grips with Foucault's voluminous and complex writings. Instead of dealing with them chronologically, however, *A Foucault Primer* concentrates on some of their central concepts, primarily Foucault's rethinking of the categories of discourse, power and the subject (or subjectivity).

'*As an introductory account designed for the non-specialist reader, this book stands out*' Paul Patton, University of Sydney

Literary Formations
Post-colonialism, nationalism, globalism
ANNE BREWSTER

Literary Formations provides a detailed examination of post-colonial literatures and literary theory. Writing from a feminist perspective, Brewster introduces the issue of gender into a field that has been widely dominated by questions of race and nationalism. She investigates the genre of Aboriginal women's autobiography and looks at the contrasting approaches to nationalism of two 'ethnic' women writers—Bharati Mukherjee in the USA and Ania Walwicz in Australia. Scrutinising the processes of neo-colonisation and the ways in which indigenous, diasporic and multicultural writing are reappropriated by the canon, *Literary Formations* is a valuable introduction to this influential area of critical thinking.

Masculinities and Identities
DAVID BUCHBINDER

Why does masculinity find itself in crisis? This book traces some causes, as well as the developing interest in masculinity and the creation of men's studies, from their origins in feminist and gay political activist theory. David Buchbinder examines the dynamics at work in various cultural constructions of masculinity, not all of which meet with approval in a patriarchal culture. The effects on men of patriarchal ideologies, phallocentrism and male sexuality (both heterosexual and homosexual) are among the issues discussed, while different strands of masculine discourse are identified and examined in a variety of texts ranging from opera to recent news stories.

'*a timely, sensible and sensitive book*' David Gilbey, Australian Book Review

Postmodern Socialism

Romanticism, City and State

PETER BEILHARZ

Injustice, poverty, living and working conditions: the attempt to deal with these social questions arose from a nineteenth-century recognition of the complex problems created mainly in cities. At the same time socialism emerged from a romantic stream of Enlightenment concerned with nature and simplicity. Socialist arguments, now widely viewed as discredited, tackled these problems that ironically remain with us in these postmodern times. By juxtaposing postmodernity and socialism we can generate illuminating perspectives on the way we live *now*. *Postmodern Socialism* traces and criticises these perspectives.

> '*an intellectual* tour de force . . . *a vital contribution to the debate on* la fin de socialisme' *Manfred Steger,* Critical Sociology

Reconstructing Theory

Gadamer, Habermas, Luhmann

EDITED BY DAVID ROBERTS

It seems that you cannot be taken seriously in critical thought these days if you are not *au fait* with the works of Foucault, Derrida and other French intellectuals. But there is an alternative tradition for those who find that deconstruction leads only to nihilism and despair.

Reconstructing Theory is an accessible and provocative introduction to the key thinkers of this alternative tradition. It investigates the contributions to social and cultural theory of Gadamer, Habermas and Luhmann, and analyses the influences of Jauss, Iser and Peter and Christa Bürger on literary theory. This book demonstrates that it may after all be possible not only to seek to explain and to criticise the world, but to humanise and even to change it.

Theories of Desire

PATRICK FUERY

Lacan, Barthes, Derrida, Foucault, Kristeva, Cixous, Irigaray: these critical theorists are all linked by their analyses of desire. *Theories of Desire* looks not only at the role of desire in the works of these writers but also examines other major issues and themes of post-structuralism. Fuery considers the place of desire in psychoanalysis, philosophy, literary studies and feminism. He highlights the connections between desire and the critical analysis of subjectivity, language and culture. He investigates the institutionalisation of desire, the relationship between language, discourse and desire, and notes the problems of dealing with women's desire in phallocentric contexts.